what
are
you
doing
after
the
orgy
?

HENNY and JIM BACKUS

illustrated by Stanton Keeney

Also by the Authors

Rocks on the Roof

Second printing .... *May, 1962*

CONTENTS

CHAPTER

1. Chicken a la King 1

2. The Magnificent Slob 13

3. Wait till it Melts 25

4. Ham on Ham 43

5. Going Fishing with the Game Warden . . 65

6. Excess Baggage 87

7. Fun and Games 97

8. Tea and Strumpets 111

9. Hey Madam—Your Sign Fell Down 127

10. What Are You Doing After the Orgy? . . . 151

11. Incident Prone 175

what are you doing after the orgy?

1 chicken a la king

HENNY AND I have always wanted to go to Europe—but when we had the money we didn't have the time—and when we had the time we didn't have the money.

I am what is known as a free lance actor, which means I am not under contract to any one studio or television network. When I finish a picture or a T.V. show I am out of work, with all the insecurities that go with being unemployed in any other job. When I'm not working, I'm not having a vacation, I'm simply out of a job.

To the average man a suntan is a badge of success. It means that everything is going well and he's been able to take off and spend a few weeks in Miami. But a Hollywood actor with a tan is suspect! We never get a chance to sit around in the sun unless we're out of work.

For example, when a movie company that has been on location making a Western epic in, say, New Mexico or Arizona returns home, the director, the camera crew, the grips, and the technicians are all the color of mahogany.

The actors who are out in the sun more than anyone else come back looking drawn and white. The explanation is very simple. The sun does not penetrate make-up. Some actors, before going on an interview for a part, will borrow their old maid aunt's rice powder and go in to see the producer looking like Kabuki dancers. We call this job insurance!

So if you're ever out in sunny Hollywood and see your favorite actor riding around in his convertible with the top up, you'll understand that he's merely trying to get a good pale.

Once when we had both the time and the money—a very rare combination in our business—we ran into a psychiatrist at a Hollywood party, where they're standard equipment (he arrived carrying a couch on his back—he'd just been making a house call), and when we told him we couldn't stand it any more and simply had to go to Europe he explained that we were running away from reality and that our behavior was immature. But everybody feels like running away once in a while—like the son of a successful movie magnate who ran away the other day. His father stormed into our house screaming,

"The kid's run away from home . . . and he's only fifteen. How do you like that?"

I tried to calm him down with some back fence philosophy.

"Take it easy, Ghengis, that's perfectly normal. Your son, Attila, is like any other teenager. All fifteen year old boys at one time or another run away from home!"

The movie tycoon glared at me and said,

"In a Thunderbird?"

At one point we decided that, with all the spare time I was racking up, we might as well come in out of the sun and write a book. Maybe if we wrote a book and got it published we would get the money to go to Europe. No one could say we were running away then! All authors go to Europe after they've launched a successful book. So why not Henny and I? . . . And that's how we came to write our first book *Rocks On The Roof*.

It was a big step when we finally sat down to put it on paper, but it wasn't until we were actually in front of the typewriter that we realized what problems confronted us. We were faced with little things like: Which tense are we in? Can you start a sentence with "and", "if" or "but"? And should we leave our participles dangling? For the first time in my life, I wished that I had paid attention in high school English class instead of spending my time testing the effects of aspirin in Coca Cola and trying to get an illicit wax mold of the key to my father's car. However, Henny must have had some native writing talent since her two-hundred-word essay, "Why I Would Like to Marry Richard Dix," is still held up as an example of hardhitting journalism and to this day is required reading for all fifth graders.

I met Henny on March 10th, 1941 at which time I was about to be locked out of my room in the Piccadilly Hotel. It was a raw, blustery day, and I had about eight cents in my pocket. Out of desperation, I went to see my agent, Herman Levin, at his home where he was confined to bed with a strange virus, probably brought on by malnutrition. Herm lived a couple of blocks away at the Hotel Royalton in exquisite squalor. I hope Mr. Levin doesn't mind these references to his humble beginnings as he is now an eminently successful Broadway producer of, for example, "My Fair Lady," and the toast of the International set. He now lives in a fabulous penthouse overlooking the East river, surrounded by his collection of paintings and nine miles of monogrammed shirts.

Herm didn't have any encouraging news for me that day, and, as we sat there commiserating with each other, there was a knock at the door. I instinctively leapt up and headed for the closet. In those days, a knock on the door meant only one thing—the credit manager.

"Take it easy," Herm said. "It's probably just that nice doll from upstairs who promised to bring me some soup."

"Herm, do you mind if I climb in bed with you? I could do with a little soup myself."

"Don't be a jerk," he replied. "I'll leave you some. Answer the door and be nice to her, Jim, she's got a hot plate."

I opened the door and there she stood, her arms outstretched, a vision of loveliness, holding a bowl of clam chowder. There was only one thing wrong. She was wearing a pair of overalls and was covered from head to foot with plaster. She handed me the bowl of soup, and in a voice that sent shivers up and down my spine, said,

"Here's the soup."

Then she disappeared down the hall in a cloud of plaster dust. I turned to Herm and said, "That's the sexiest-looking bricklayer I ever saw."

"Bricklayer?" replied Herm. "Oh, you mean the plaster. She's a sculptress. Her name is Henriette Kaye and she acts, too. She is also a successful model. That's why she's got so much soup up there."

What's the use of kidding? I was smitten, though I never believed it could happen. It was a case of love at first sight.

Shortly after, Henny and I decided to get married. We dreamed of a honeymoon trip to Europe—we kept dreaming of that honeymoon trip to Europe for nineteen years! Though we'd had our share of connubial bliss, we felt that until we connubed in a ship's stateroom, on the rooftops of Paris, and in a gondola in Venice, we hadn't connubed at all!

During the two years it took us to write the book, I used

to say things to her like, "Boy, wait'll this book is published. Then we'll really go to Europe—the right way! First of all we'll go to Paris for a year. They can send our royalty checks there. Then the following year, Majorca. I was talking to John O'Hara, and he told me they can forward your royalty checks anywhere in the world. No! —Maybe—let's go to Capri!! I can see us now—coming ashore in our little tirene—you, brown as a berry in a bikini, with those rope soles—and me in a Basque shirt and earrings. Say, maybe I'll go native and have my ears pierced!!!"

"Right now," snapped my wife, "you sound gay enough to have your wrists pierced. Now c'mon lover—let's try to write this book—Europe comes later!"

Well, Europe came much later! *Rocks on the Roof* was written. It was accepted by the publisher. It came out in late October of 1958. It was launched on "This Is Your Life." It got fine notices. It did very well . . . but our work on that book did not really start until it was on sale at your neighborhood bookstore.

Right after "This Is Your Life," we introduced the book on a very dignified T.V. show which I think was called "Authors and Critics Roundtable." We had to go clear to North Dakota to do it, but all the time and expense was worthwhile as it accounted for a substantial number of sales—the royalties of which might have almost bought the cork soles.

We were studying travel folders for our trip to Europe one night, when the phone rang. It turned out to be Mrs. Campbell, who, with her husband, owns Campbell's Book Store, one of the biggest in Los Angeles. She said,

"Jimmy, if you and Henny want your book to sell, you've got to do something for me. The Rotary Anns are having a luncheon three weeks from Monday at the Beverly Hills Hotel and they specifically asked for you and

Henny to go and say a few words to them. Now, you can't turn me down!"

"Well," I stalled, "we did have some plans to . . ."

"Now, Jimmy," she exploded, "you have to do this! If the Rotary Anns want you, you have to come! It means a great deal to your book!"

"Oh . . . well," I said. "Why didn't you tell me . . . the Rotary Anns! Of course! . . . If I had known in the first place . . . the Rotary Anns . . . well, now . . . naturally, I'll get Henny and do it!!! But tell me one thing, Mrs. Campbell . . . who the hell are the Rotary Anns?"

She explained that the Rotary Anns are the ladies' auxiliary of the Rotary Club, which goes to prove that if you ask a foolish question, you get a foolish answer.

The day of the luncheon my wife was perfectly groomed in her new suit, her chic hat, and her little white gloves. If you were casting a movie for the part of a successful authoress who was about to address a ladies' club, you might have said that Henny was too much the type. As for me, I had on my dark blue suit, my sincere tie, and a pearl-gray fedora. I turned to Henny and said:

"How do I look?"

"You're dressed perfectly for a man who's on his way to speak at a ladies luncheon. There's just one thing—one little thing—take off those earrings!"

If you'll forgive my modesty, we were a mild sensation. The ladies loved us. I told stories about Henny. She told stories about me. Every time she got up to talk I gave her a playful little pat on the fanny—and they loved it! They howled at everything we said and everything we did. They were a great audience—to say the least. If the ladies loved us, we, in turn, loved the ladies. Just as we and the eighty women were relaxing over our coffee and getting to know each other, Mrs. Campbell got up and announced that she just happened to have some copies of *Rocks On*

The Roof with her and that if they bought one we would be happy to autograph same. At this point she pulled a gigantic carton of books from underneath a table. And from beneath her stole she produced one of those belts that street car conductors used to have to make change, and those Rotary Anns, bless their little flowered heads, stood in line and bought one hundred and twenty copies of our book. Not bad! Eighty ladies—and they bought one hundred and twenty copies.

Well, the next morning Mr. Campbell called and said:

"Listen, Jim, you kids were such a smash with the Rotary Anns, the men are going to have a stag luncheon. Three hundred members of the Rotary Club, some of whose wives you met the other day—and they're dying to have you speak!"

I said:

"O.K., I'll be there!"

Now, I was getting greedy! My mind started going like an adding machine. I figured if eighty Rotary Anns buy one hundred and twenty copies, think what three hundred Rotarians would buy. Mind you—these are the guys who control the purse strings in the family. I grabbed the phone and dialed Mr. Campbell:

"Say, listen," I said. "It just occurred to me these are the husbands of the ladies who bought all those books—so let's be prepared. Bring plenty of sales slips, lots of change, and you'd better back up a van full of books."

Well, I spoke at the luncheon, and a performer knows when he's good and when he's bad. And all I can say is that I was a trifle more than magnificent! I must have been because I was inspired thinking about selling all those books!

After my performance, the chairman requested them to give me three "Hi, Jim's," which consisted of the entire membership rising to their feet as one and chanting in full throated unison, "Hi, Jim—Hi, Jim—Hi, Jim"—and which in bullfighting circles would be the equivalent to both ears, the tail, and maybe a hoof or two. Mr. Campbell then announced that the book was for sale, and that I would be happy to autograph them for all who cared to buy. He brought out his crates of books, set up shop . . . and we waited.

You know how many books we sold to those three hundred wildly cheering Rotarians? THREE!#$%@@&! Now don't misunderstand me! If I had gotten up and told them I had an uncle who needed an operation and didn't have the dough, they'd have knocked each other down trying to hand me money. But books—no! We learned our first lesson in the luncheon book business. And we pass this tip on to all embryonic authors. *Men* just don't buy books!! Booze, yes! Books, no!!

If we had any intentions of going to Europe, from that time on we had to forget it. We were booked for luncheons! It was one luncheon after another! If you want to be an author nowadays, you'd better be prepared to hit what we call the "Chicken a la King" circuit. Some luncheons we both attended. Some, Henny couldn't make. And some, vice versa. There was one occasion where we both were unable to make it, so they played a tape of our voices.

The hotel rooms, the restaurants, the cities and the ladies all changed. But the cast of authors with whom we were on the circuit remained the same as long as their books stayed on the best seller list. It was like being in vaudeville thirty years ago. There we sat, day after day, the same authors smiling at each other over mountains of cantaloup balls, rivers of consommé, glaciers of tomato aspic and those little patties, which soon began to seem like tiny volcanoes about to erupt molten chicken lava. There we sat smiling at each other over those same speeches. We all knew each other's talks by heart. I'm sure they got as sick of ours as we did of theirs.

There was one cheerful fellow who had written a book about that popular subject of today, "Togetherness," with projects for the whole household like, "How to Build Your Own Swamp—Or The Family that Drinks Together Stays Together!"

There was the stock market analyst who had written a fascinating volume called *How To Increase Your Income —Or Up Your Bracket!* He was a big smash until he read his title on a national network!

There was the wife of a political figure who had written a pseudo-spiritual tome called, *I Made Love To A Bear For The F.B.I.—And Found God!*

There were also a number of authors who came and went, replacing those of us whose books had slipped. There were authors of new books with titles like *Where Is Europe?*—a brilliant exposé of the unprincipled methods of map makers the world over . . .

And *Blind Love Is Not*, the sophisticated swift-moving vignette of wartime Trenton . . .

And *Organ Exercises for Four Hands*, which was a very valuable book for those who were lucky enough to have four hands.

As we remember it, those of us who lasted out the tour were Elick Moll and his *Seidman and Son*, Sheilah Graham and her *Beloved Infidel*, and Pappy Boyington and his *Baa Baa Black Sheep*, whose speeches we never tired of. His opening line was, "I'm Pappy Boyington . . . and I'm a drunk!" which caused the sea of ladies' hats to flutter like a cyclone hitting a petunia bed. He followed that up with "Show me a hero . . . and I'll show you a bum!!" which shook the ladies to their very foundations . . . and I do mean foundations!

For some reason the publishers of *Rocks On The Roof* left Henny's name off the cover of the book, and since the story was about both of us and obviously written by both of us, no one was ever able to understand it. So to straighten it out here and now, let me assure you that Henny collaborated with me! Again, I say,

TO HENNY
With whom I collaborated all the time.
She also helped me write that book.

CHAPTER

2 the magnificent slob

THIS IS HENNY——

My husband, Jimmy, is sloppy, disorganized, vague, preoccupied, distraught and undisciplined. Yet he arrives at his destination in life as though it were carefully charted. He's the most meticulously confused person I have ever met . . . but I love him, and I always have . . . ever since our eyes first met over that steaming bowl of soup.

I don't think he ever proposed to me. He sort of took things for granted, and it wasn't until we were on a train for Philadelphia that he told me we were on our way to get married. We had a glorious honeymoon—on the day coach coming back. And 48 ecstatic hours later, I couldn't believe my ears when he said:

"What do you say we get married?"

"*What you say?*" I shrieked. "What did we do in Philadelphia . . . get a dog license?"

"Now, wait a minute, honey," he said, giving me my first taste of pure Backus logic.

13

"We did it in Philadelphia for your family. Now the least we can do is get married again in Cleveland for mine. Then, when we're through in Cleveland, we can do it in Pittsburgh for my Aunt Geneva . . . and then we can go to . . ."

"Wait a minute," I cried. "Wait a minute. I'm willing to be a blushing bride again for your family, but if you think for one minute that I'm going to take our marriage on tour . . ."

"Okay," agreed Jimmy, "I'll wire the Cleveland tribe and we can leave tomorrow right after the party."

"What party?" I asked.

"The party I persuaded Kay Thompson to give to celebrate our marriage," stated Jimmy.

I was horrified! "You asked Kay to give us a party?"

"Well," he said, "We're doing the radio show together every week. It's the least she can do."

Jim feels that working closely with someone he likes creates a mystic bond. If he had his own way, he would go through the complete Indian rite of blood brotherhood. I didn't understand this at the time, but a party was a party, and who was I to complain.

"About the tickets," I wondered, "how do you know we can get train space on such short notice?"

"Oh, that," smiled Jim. "That's very simple. You see," he continued once again with his special brand of logic, "there's only one man to get the tickets—Alec Wilder. He gets railroad tickets better than anyone in the world. He'd be honored to get them, so don't worry. We'll be on that train tomorrow night."

Well, I guess I had better explain about the ticket-buying-Mr. Wilder, who at that time I barely knew. Alec Wilder, who is considered one of America's foremost composers, has a very strange hobby. He's train happy and is never without his *Railroad Guide,* (a phonebook-sized volume) which he studies in every spare moment. He's so crazy about trains that in 1938 he took a little time off and went to California on one hundred and sixty-five different lines. Of course, I couldn't imagine why any grown man would want to go to Grand Central Station and stand in line for hours to buy two tickets to Cleveland, but to Jim it was perfectly natural to assume that Alec would be delighted . . . and he was.

The next afternoon at Kay's, as six o'clock drew near, I began to get a little nervous. You see, the train left at eight and there was no sign of Mr. Wilder and those tickets. At six-thirty, just as I was about to have a quiet fit, Alec came in the door. Jim, in his relaxed way, said,

"Did you get the tickets, Alec?"

"Certainly," said Alec, as he began to go through the pockets of his giant overcoat, which incidentally, he wears at all times and in all seasons, indoors as well as out. He started scrabbling through it. Mr. Wilder, besides never being without his huge overcoat and his king-sized railroad guide, always has on his person, eight or nine out of town newspapers, numerous musical score sheets, memos to himself written on anything that was handy at the time, and four or five new time-tables he is currently studying. My heart was in my mouth while Alec spent a good ten minutes going through his endless pockets.

No tickets!

"Well," he said, "I'd better have a drink." Jim agreed wholeheartedly and both dear boys went off to the bar.

Jim's exit line that I heard through the rushing sound in my ears was, "Alec, you certainly deserve one."

A half-hour and three drinks later, Alec was still sorting papers with no sign of a ticket and I was going crazy. Not only were we going to miss the train, but we were out a couple of hundred dollars. Jim calmly took all this in his stride and whispered to me, "Look, sweetie, I know Alec, so please don't worry."

He turned to Alec, who was up to his neck in trash and whom I would have loved to kill, and said, "Alec, sit down quietly over here. Relax. Now, think. The tickets. The last time you saw them! Think back . . . now, think, Alec."

Alec closed his eyes and went into a semi-trance. "The tickets," he droned. "I remember I bought them. I was walking through the lobby of the Vanderbilt Hotel when I saw him . . . a man in a large fedora with a three-year-old boy who looked like Tom Mix. They intrigued me. I sat down."

With this, he jumped nine feet in the air and shouted, "I've got it! They're under the vase! That hideous porcelain vase. The one that shows the Pharoah shooting the elk. I put them there for safekeeping!"

This did it for me, and I blew my stack at Jimmy's dear friend.

"Tickets . . . underneath a vase in the Vanderbilt! You must be an idiot!!! Don't you know that anyone can steal them? They're as good as cash! What makes you think they're still there?"

Sweetly, Alec replied, "Honey, believe me those tickets are still there. That vase is so hideous no one ever goes near it . . . only me. It's the only place where I can be completely alone."

"You see, sweetie," said my brand new spouse, "aren't you sorry you made such a fuss? I knew Alec wouldn't let us down."

Twenty minutes later, after the longest cab ride of my life, we stopped in front of the Vanderbilt. Jimmy went in and came directly out, calm and smiling, with both tickets clutched in his hand. Ten minutes later we were on the train for Cleveland.

This theme with many, many variations has been re-peated and repeated each time we planned a trip of any sort—especially that trip to Europe!

And so we were married again! This time at the home of Jim's sister, Kate, and his brother-in-law, Jock Spencer. We were even greater than before, naturally, since this is the only marriage I know of that had an out-of-town tryout! Now, for the first time, I saw the Backus family in action. They operate much the same as General Motors. It's a large corporation, but each is a separate unit, like Pontiac, Buick, and Oldsmobile. I am sure this is one wedding the minister will never forget. Not only was this the first ceremony he had ever performed, but after it was over, Jim's mother, knowing his father was absent-minded, took the minister aside and gave him twenty dollars. Jim's father, knowing his mother never carried any money, took the minister aside and gave him twenty dollars. Jim's sister, knowing her parents very well, took the minister aside and gave him twenty dollars. Jim's grandmother, overcome by three glasses of champagne, took the min-ister aside and gave him twenty dollars. Jim, feeling re-sponsible for the whole thing, took the minister aside and gave him twenty dollars. Jock, who considered the Backuses guests in his home, took the minister aside and gave him twenty dollars, and I, having fallen in love with my new family, took it upon myself to take the minister aside and give him twenty dollars.

I can honestly say that Jimmy is one husband who never forgets a birthday or an anniversary. He loves to buy me presents. He loves to buy me luxurious presents that I would never buy for myself. You bet I wouldn't! Like the black ostrich feather mules, the red maribou negligee, the lace opera hose with rhinestone clocks, the black garters trimmed with ermine tails, and the bedside incense burner!! Once I got up enough nerve to ask him about them.

"Darling, where do you get the ideas for those lovely presents you give me?"

"That's very simple," he answered, "I merely describe you to the salesladies."

I don't know—maybe I should slap his face. He must describe me as a dame who once lived on the Barbary Coast, whose house was not a home!

Every so often he throws me a curve. One day, shortly after we came to Hollywood in 1946, we were taking a leisurely drive in Jim's brand new beloved car—the first car of his own since he left Cleveland. Suddenly, we both saw the most beautiful mink coat in the world in the window of an exclusive fur shop. I didn't dare say a word, but Jimmy stopped the car and said,

"Let's go in, baby, and you can try it on."

"But how?" I asked. "We haven't got a dime."

"Never mind," said Jimmy, "let's just see how it looks."

He didn't have to coax me, and in we went. It looked good. It felt good. It even smelled good. As I stood there drooling, Jimmy asked how much it was.

"Six thousand dollars . . . and tax," replied the furrier. I almost fainted.

"You have to pay one-third down before you can take it," he continued, "it's a Federal law."

"Wait a minute," said my husband, "I'll be right back."

I couldn't imagine what he had in mind but I waited, never for a moment taking off the divinely beautiful coat. After two hours, I began to get a little nervous and finally, because of the strange looks darted my way by the furrier and his staff, I reluctantly took off "my coat" and started for the phone, when in came a beaming Jimmy. He gave them the down payment and signed the papers. I walked out into the June sunshine wearing the most beautiful mink coat in the world.

"Jimmy," I gasped, "how did you do it?"

"I'll tell you later, baby," he said, "but first I've got to call us a cab."

That was the same year he gave me an electric pencil sharpener for Valentine's Day. You've got to admit he keeps me off balance.

When it comes to feeding Jim, however, I maintain an even keel. I have always loved to cook. I've made a study of it, and I consider it an art and a pleasure. When we were first married, Jim had no excuse to do any of the burnt-bride-biscuit jokes. He could never have said that ours was the only garbage disposal unit in the world that had to take bicarbonate of soda, or that pygmies came every year to dip their darts in my stew. It took Jim a long time to get used to my idea of a meal because, when it comes to cooking, Jim, due to his Cleveland background, is of the traditional midwestern, bread-basket-of-the-nation school of eating. I guess through the years I have helped turn Jim into a "fair-to-middlin'" gourmet. On holidays, however, I don't fool around. Come Thanksgiving and Christmas, our table looks like a painting by Grandma Moses. On Easter, he wants colored hard-boiled eggs and a ham, and on the Fourth of July, I had better serve him hot dogs, potato salad, corn on the cob, brick ice cream shaped like an American flag and a pitcher of lemonade.

A few years ago we invited some old friends to our first Thanksgiving dinner in our new home. I thought it might be fun to do something a little different. A week before the holiday, I told Jimmy that I was going to barbecue a boned turkey in honey and soy sauce. Instead of creamed onions and sweet potatoes, I was going to serve Chinese show peas and water chestnuts, and, in place of cranberries, I had ordered some preserved cumquats. Jim looked at me as though I had just told him I was planning to put a time bomb under the White House.

When I place an unknown dish in front of Jim, he always looks up at me and says, "Is this any good?"

I give him the adult version of, "Look at mama . . . she's eating it," and "num, num, it's good." It always works. I have even toyed with the idea of putting slightly pornographic pictures at the bottom of his dish. When he is especially dubious about a new concoction he asks me the big question,

"How much would this cost in Chasen's?"

I might say, "Four dollars and thirty-five cents a portion."

He starts to eat and stops. "Is that with the vegetables or without?"

"Oh, no," I assure him. "The artichoke souffle is a buck twenty-five apiece, and the salad would be about two-forty and you'd have to tip Bill at least two dollars for mixing and tossing it, and don't forget I'm giving you a pony of brandy with the coffee that would have to come to around three dollars. Darling, if we were eating this dinner at Chasen's it would cost at least thirty-two dollars, and don't forget you haven't tipped the guy for getting the car. So think of the money I've saved you."

With this he eats the dinner beaming to think of how clever he is and how much money he saved. By this method, one gourmet was made!

He is also equally as easily pleased by clothes. They can sell him anything. Fortunately nowadays either the studio tells him what to wear or he consults his tailor. Even there I have to watch him, for though he patronizes one of the finest tailors in town, even the tailor is human. He may have gotten stuck with a bolt of purple llama wool, and guess who would be his only customer for a topcoat of same?

Speaking of topcoats, when I first met Jim he was wearing a coat of irridescent green that changed colors, according to the light, and it wasn't until we had been married for three months that I persuaded him to start the fire with it.

The finest garment he almost bought was in a shop in New York. He went in to buy a suit and found one. The salesman assured him it was just for him. Above the protests of the entire personnel, he called me up and asked me to come right over to approve it. When I got there I saw him preening himself in front of the triple mirror, resplendent in a suit of white gabardine with pink satin lapels. Needless to say, my pigeon was wearing one of the suits that had been made for the bongo player in a thirty-two piece rhumba band who had just eloped with Lucille Ball.

Next to the farmer, I guess the motion picture performer is the earliest riser. For the movie actress, the average studio call is seven o'clock in make-up. For the fortunate actor, the call is seven-thirty or, at the latest, eight. On location, the calls are usually an hour to an hour-and-a-half earlier. For example, when Jimmy was making "It Happened One Night" with June Allyson in Tucson, Arizona, they had to be driven every morning from the hotel to the location spot, sixty-five miles away. Jim had a late call because he wore no make-up. He didn't have to get up till five-thirty a.m. They never finished shooting until about six at night, and then made the same long drive back to the hotel, which brought them in about seven-thirty. This gives you some idea of the hours that go into the making of a movie. I roughly figured that Jimmy has made sixty-two pictures, plus five years of filming two weekly television shows, all of which amounts to approximately forty-five hundred mornings when he had to get up between six and six-thirty a.m. every day.

You'd think he'd get in the habit of early rising, but not my boy. The minute he has a day off, he reverts right back to his New York habit of sleeping till noon. Then, when he gets his next early call, he behaves as though it had never happened before. He goes into a state of utter panic. He has an early dinner of consommé, a lean lamb chop and a cup of cocoa. After dinner comes an hour or so of music and meditation. We then coordinate and set all five of his alarm clocks and alert his telephone waking service. At nine-thirty he's in his "blasting off for the moon" outfit. This consists of soft flannel pajamas with built-in feet, an eye mask, ear plugs, and the controls of the electric blanket clutched in his hand. He looks like he belongs in the window of Lewis and Conger. After a final glass of warm milk—lights out! Utter silence and woe betide me if I make a sound. Naturally we have separate bedrooms because with all his paraphernalia, there isn't much room for me.

Also, needless to say, there isn't much time for connubial bliss. The only chance for connubing is when he's out of work, but then he's such a hysterical wreck, he spends all his waking moments phoning his agent. (I really shouldn't tell you this, but instead of a teddy bear he sleeps with his arms wrapped around a nine iron.)

Well, to get back to lover boy. At nine-fifty p.m. I can tell by the tones of his gentle snoring that he is sound asleep. At one-thirty he's wide awake—and furious. He tries every known method of getting back to sleep. Lying perfectly still, listening to soft music, thinking of beautiful flowers, assuming the lotus position, are to no avail. He gets out of bed enraged, maligning the motion picture industry, threatening to go into another business, and, of course, blaming his agent. Then at six-fifteen he drifts into sleep again, only to be awakened fifteen minutes later by the five alarms and the phone service.

And now it takes a bit of doing to get him off to his studio. Willa, our housekeeper, and I pour coffee down his throat until he comes to. Then, once fully awake, he becomes very pompous and businesslike. He bids us a formal good morning, dresses, kisses me on the cheek and is out the door. It never fails. It's the same every morning. Willa and I stand there and count slowly to five . . . he bursts in. He's forgotten something . . . the car keys! He kisses me again and is off. We count five. He's back again . . . the script! He leaves. It averages four or five of these before he is thoroughly gone. Then Willa and I wearily go to bed as we haven't had a wink of sleep all night long.

I must explain that . . . well . . . I guess I've told a few tales out of school, and . . . well . . . maybe I've exaggerated a little. He's really a darling and I love him very much. I'm getting pretty sentimental as I sit here in the quiet of my room. It's well after midnight and I've been reminiscing all this time, thinking back on all the lovely years that . . . oh, no! The howling and groaning . . . that terrible thrashing . . . oh, no! Another sleepless night . . .

CHAPTER

3 wait till it melts

THIS IS JIM——

One of the advantages of being a motion picture actor nowadays is going on location. I always dreamed of going on a good long European location and taking Henny—like, maybe to Paris, or the Riviera or the Greek islands. What a way to have that glamorous honeymoon I'd promised her . . . all expenses paid!!

I remember once playing golf with Victor Mature. It was a memorable round, as Vic hit Dean Martin just as he was about to take a shot . . . knocked the bottle clean out his hand! Vic had just returned from making a picture in Holland and when he finished the eighteen, I said,

"Vic, let's play next week."

"Love to, Jim," he said, "But I don't know when I'll be back. I've got four pictures lined up. First I go to Italy, then I have one in the Kenya Colony, then I go to England and then in February we are shooting in the Caribbean."

May I say I drooled with envy. Most of the pictures I had made were shot at the studio in and around Los Angeles, and once, one glamorous week, in Philadelphia. To make it even more exotic, Philadelphia is Henny's home town. So to please Henny I stayed with one of her numerous relatives. I'm the only actor who ever went on location and lived in. With toting privileges.

Finally the spell was broken. My agent, Billy Josephy, called me and said,

"Jim, I just got you a picture at Warner Brothers. You'd better start packing because they're gonna make it on location and you're leaving in two days, and—hold on to your hat—you'd better get ready for a nice long trip!"

"A long trip!" I thought happily. "Could it be? At last?" I just finished reading where seventy per cent of our pictures were being shot in Europe because of frozen funds. Little did I realize how frozen . . . because the picture turned out to be "Ice Palace," which is the story of two families. Only instead of the dynasties living in Texas like they do in "Giant," they live in Alaska, and instead of the heir marrying a Mexican, the heiress marries an Eskimo. "Ice Palace" is really "Giant" on the rocks.

Henny couldn't go because she refuses to fly, and anyway it didn't sound like honeymoon material to her . . . or for that matter to either of us. Attached to the script was a list of instructions.

Vincent Sherman—Director   27th July
"ICE PALACE"—#854
LOCATION INFORMATION SHEET

Locations:
The Warner Bros. location unit will be working on two (2) different location sites in Alaska, as follows:

Petersburg, Alaska (1st location)
Headquarters for the Company will be in the Mitkof Hotel

which is located in Petersburg. The weather is similar to that of San Francisco.

Point Barrow, Alaska (2nd location)
At this location personnel will work in cold weather, snow and ice. The temperature is around 40° to 50° during the daytime and below freezing in the evening. It is suggested to all personnel to bring *very warm* clothing for this location.

Length of Stay:
The length of stay for both locations will be approximately twenty-one (21) days, including travel.

Accommodations:
All accommodations will be the best obtainable in each of the two locations. In Petersburg and Point Barrow the accommodations are extremely limited.

Baggage:
It is requested that all personnel limit their baggage to two (2) pieces. Please keep in mind the various types of climate at the locations, and it is suggested that only practical, warm clothing be taken to the locations. (Limit:—40 lbs.)

Insurance:
Be sure each individual has been signed up for flight insurance.

Work calls, etc.:
All personnel will be responsible for their own wakeup calls. Bring alarm clocks.

Daily work and leaving calls will be determined on the location. All calls for following day's work will be given at the end of each day's work on the location. If changes are made in the evening, a responsible person at each lodging will notify personnel.

No overtime or meal penalties will be honored unless previously okayed by Unit Manager.

Purchase of supplies or rental of local equipment must be okayed by Unit Manager before taking action.

Transportation to Location:
All personnel will travel from Los Angeles via United Air
Lines Flight No. 771, departing from International Airport at
5:45 P.M., arrive Seattle, Washington at 8:10 P.M. All personnel will stay *overnight* in Seattle. Leave Seattle at 7:00 A.M.
the following morning via Pacific Northern Airlines for Annette Island, arriving at 9:40 A.M. Leave Annette Island at
11:00 A.M. for Petersburg, Alaska via Ellis Air Lines arriving
at 12:15 P.M.

As the company was already shooting in Alaska, I was
to proceed and join them. I will never forget that day in
July when I left. Henny drove me to International Airport
and just before we took off, she placed a volume of Robert
W. Service in my hand, parted my parka, and rubbed her
cold little nose against mine.

Warners had chosen the quaint little town of Petersburg
as the locale. To get there you first had to go to Seattle,
where the studio with its usual loving foresight had arranged for me to spend the night in the Men's room.
Early the next morning we took off in a strange looking
plane. I don't know how old it was. All I can tell you is
that I found Lindbergh's lunch under my seat.

In five hours we put down on a remote landing strip
called Annette Island, which from the air looked like
Georgie Jessel's toupee at low tide. The airport at Annette was a pine-panelled room full of burnt-leather Indian pillows, wampum lamp shades, and polar bear throw
rugs. It resembled the recreation hall at a summer resort
in the Catskill mountains. Welcome to Annette, cha, cha,
cha!

After a comfort station stop at Annette I was bundled
into a Grumman Amphibious Goose—a tin plane which
looks like a flying lunch box. This flight was delightfully
informal, as, once airborne, the pilot announced over a
Rudy Vallee megaphone!

"Welcome aboard! This is Captain Peary speaking. We will be flying at an altitude of thirty-eight feet. This flight will be non-stop unless somebody waves. Please remain in your seat until I have put out my foot and brought the plane to a complete stop."

Four hours and seven new passengers later, our plane landed in the water at the Petersburg airport. The Petersburg airport is a tall thin wharf jutting out into the water about a quarter of a mile. Our luggage and ourselves were hauled out of a plane by a local girl sporting a butch haircut and wearing army shoes. She tossed us into a tiny Volkswagen bus, and now came the dangerous part of the trip. This Northern beauty drove us at breakneck speed down the slippery planks of the wharf, which was at best eight feet wide with no railings and a good 40 feet above the icy water.

Petersburg is a fishing village, just reaching its fiftieth year and flanking the shores of Wrangell Narrows. This town is so small that the city limit signs are back to back. It is populated by almost two thousand people, but somehow the population always remains the same—whenever somebody has a baby, someone has to leave town. It has extreme tides of from twenty-five to thirty feet and since it was low tide at the time, the whole town appeared to be on stilts. And here I quote from the March issue of *The Alaska Sportsman*, page 38, in describing Petersburg.

"There is also the smell of steaming shrimp boiling pink in the vats, of piles of butter clams, shells freshly opened, of great slabs of red king salmon slowly smoking in the slatted towers, from which come thin tendrils of Aldar smoke, of black cod, which are only black on the skin and white as snow within, kippering on the same racks beside the fat king, salting down in great round tierces for other smoking later."

Remember this is a quote! Even the Chamber of Commerce admits this city has an air about it.

After checking into the Mitkof Hotel I decided to get into my dangerous Dan McGrew outfit and take a walk around the town. On my way out, the man at the desk informed me that our company was still shooting some fishing scenes out at sea and wouldn't be back for several hours. I was no sooner out of the hotel when I almost got a ticket for jaywalking. I hadn't observed the mush and don't mush signals.

I looked around me. The main street which was one block long consisted of the business establishments necessary to supply the needs of any normal community—a market, a bank, a drug store, a trading post, a dress shop featuring cardboard mannequins, and so forth. There was, however, the addition of one large store which sold vicious looking traps, a murderous assortment of guns, a terrifying array of harpoons of various sizes, and which had as its conversation piece, a nine foot tall stuffed polar bear, fangs bared and ready to spring. For a moment I thought I was in John Wayne's living room! And, oh yes, there was a barber shop with a sign in the window which read, "Gone to Seattle." It never said when the barber had left, how long he would be gone, when he was coming back, if ever, or "go take a shave for yourself." What am I saying? This was not like any other normal community. Among other things every single place of business, including the bank, and even the jail and the library, had juke boxes which blared forth "rock and roll" twenty-four hours a day.

I was having a wonderful time seeing the sights of this colorful little city, when, for some unknown reason I began to feel uneasy. I couldn't imagine why! Suddenly it dawned on me! I was the only one in the town who was dressed like a sourdough. All the natives were wearing suits like perfectly normal men in a perfectly normal small town. Some of them had on Madison Avenue business suits tucked into rubber boots. The majority of the women, however, were wearing yellow slickers which gave the place a "John Held, Jr." air. It wasn't until much later that I found out that the slickers were the uniform of the day, if you worked in a cannery cleaning fish, and almost every woman did. Rumor has it that they had a beauty contest up there and nobody won. There was one girl, though, who had early American features—she looked like a buffalo.

There was an additional reason for my uneasiness. I was used to being recognized. This was the first time in about ten years that I wasn't. (The series I did for so many years, "I Married Joan," is now in its eighth showing from coast to coast, and I've appeared on just about every major television network in the country, and am currently doing my own "Jim Backus" show.) The people in Petersburg don't have television and, thanks to the mountains, they can't even get radio reception. They had never seen me in a movie because their lone little movie theater showed only vintage films, to say the least. So instead of being asked, "What is Jack Paar really like?" they later asked me, "What is Jack Hoxie really like?"

To put it mildly, I was disappointed. Was this what I had traveled two thousand miles due north to see? Where were the characters I had read about in Jack London—the grizzled bearded sons of the Yukon, the mesh stockinged belles that Wilson Mizener wrote about? This place looked like Fire Island with icebergs.

I was walking along dejectedly when suddenly my heart lifted. There in the distance coming toward me was a band of forty or fifty true Alaskans—tall, bearded huskies wearing the traditional red-and-black checked mackinaws, sealskin boots, and gaily-knitted stocking caps. As they marched along shouting and singing bawdy songs, they passed among them a bottle, meanwhile indulging in playful eye-gouging and crotch-kicking, while at the same time tossing from one to the other a fur-clad Eskimo girl to be savagely embraced. They were carrying all the gear of the North country—harpoons to rend the whale blubber, great axes to cleave the virgin pine, and kayaks still dripping brine. As they drew closer I noticed they were also carrying cables, lights, reflectors, cameras and the fur-clad Eskimo girl was clutching her script-girl's script. You see, the movie company always looks more so than the natives.

I joined the happy throng and Richard Burton suggested that I meet him in his room for a drink. Mr. Burton, as befitted a star of his caliber, was occupying the "Balto" suite, K-9. The "Balto" suite overlooked the harbor, or should I say overhung the harbor. Actually, it projected out over the water for about twenty feet, and only a giant wooden tee kept the whole thing from dropping into the inlet. This suite had two windows, one on each side of the room. One had a view of the incredibly beautiful snow-capped mountains rimming the waters of Wrangell Narrows and the other looked out on a decaying steam engine.

We were busy pouring out drinks when suddenly the entire room shook. This shaking was accompanied by an ominous gnawing sound. Much to our dismay an iceberg was nuzzling against the side of Mr. Burton's suite and a large jagged piece of it was protruding through the open window nearly decapitating our director, Vincent Sherman. Richard Burton, with typical English aplomb, stalked through the door to the top of the stairs and in his best Shakespearean tone bellowed, "I say there, Room Service!! I know we ordered ice . . . but *this* is ridiculous!!"

Now came the biggest problem of the day—where to have dinner. Apparently there was no place left. They had already tried all the eating places on Main Street, where they fried everything in Vaseline. About then, Robert Ryan came into Richard's room with the news that he'd discovered a wonderful restaurant about five miles out of town. With all the naiveté of the new man just up from the states, I said,

"Five miles . . . how will we ever get there?" Everyone shot me a "How can you be so stupid?" look and said in unison, "We'll hail a cab!!!"

The most amazing thing about Petersburg is the taxi situation. Here is a town of not quite two thousand people, accessible only by seaplane and steamer, and mind you on an island, with only eighteen miles of gravel or dirt road which leads absolutely nowhere, and yet there were two rival taxi companies and each doing a thriving business. At any hour of the day or night (it was day nineteen hours out of twenty-four up there), you would see five or six cabs just cruising around the streets. I remember one Sunday morning—it was 5:00 A.M. to be exact—Richard and I were having a nightcap cigarette in the Mitkof lobby after working all night.

"Richard, just look out there . . . one cab after another, people waving bottles and laughing and singing like it was New Year's Eve. Last week I left New York, where I was doing the Dave Garroway show. I had a 5:30 rehearsal every morning, and it took a bellboy twenty to thirty minutes at that hour to find me a cab. And this, I want you to know, was in New York! While here in this little town in Alaska we could walk out this door and snap our fingers and two cabs would be standing there."

"I know, old boy," said Richard, "but after we hailed them, where would we go?"

Funny thing, we never solved the mystery. The whole town just seemed to have a cab fetish.

The most unforgettable character I ever met, if the *Reader's Digest* will pardon the expression, was the lady cab driver who became our personal chauffeur. She also owned the cab company. Her name was Lola. Lola was a giant of a woman who talked exactly like Gypsy Rose Lee—that same sibilant, straight-woman delivery. She slept in her cab stand. That was her home. Her chauffeur's uniform consisted of a very short, skin-tight black satin sheath, white canvas wedgies and a mackinaw. This costume was topped off by a huge handbag which was full to bursting with silver dollars, and she carried it slung over her shoulder on a rope. I once saw her fell a brawling lumberman at six paces with this lethal reticule.

Lola became our constant companion, guide, confidante, Louella Parsons, and bodyguard. One night I was buying Lola some refreshments at a sidewalk bar in front of one of the town's tonier bistros. It was the stroke of midnight and we were having a drink and getting some sun when, out of nowhere, an Indian crazed with alcohol lurched at me with a drawn knife. He mumbled something about me and his squaw and hanky-panky in his teepee. I am not exaggerating. This crazed aborigine whom I had never seen before in my life was ready to stab me! As he was about to make Shish Kebab out of me, Lola let fly with a handbag hook to the chops that sent him reeling, at the same time admonishing him with, "Royal, I'm ashamed of you. You're a bad Indian."

With this she gave him another prod with her purse.

"You know you shouldn't drink! You should be ashamed. You ought to join Fire Water Anonymous! How many times have I told you that! Mr. Backus is a nice actor. He's up here making a picture. What will they think of you in Hollywood when he goes back there and tells them how you're behaving!"

At this point she gave him a low sizzler to his jockey shorts.

"Mr. Backus never even met your wife! You forget! You're so drunk all the time. Zza Zza left you and went to the mainland over a month ago."

After a few more swipes with her powerful pouch and admonishments delivered in her best Gypsy Rose Lee style, Lola sent a chastened Indian scurrying down the street, and calmly returned to her unfinished Pink Lady.

With or without our bodyguard Lola, going to any of the local bars was really living dangerously. This was the height of the fishing season, and all the saloons were full of juiced-up anglers. Everyone always thinks of a professional fisherman as a kindly, grizzled old tar, clad in oilskins, smoking an upside-down corncob pipe, sitting on a coil of rope, and whittling a ship the hard way—inside the bottle. The fishermen of Petersburg were a very different breed of cat. These men were not permanent residents of the town, as fishing for salmon is seasonal and the crews come from all walks of life. Most of them were tough young kids from the four corners of the globe, although a few were college students, and I met one or two who were professors. There were Indians, Asiatics and Eskimos, and a handful of European wildmen who looked like they were on a sabbatical from the French Foreign Legion. They all had a single purpose, to make a fast buck—and that they did.

The canning companies paid 75¢ a fish. The average fishing boat consisted of a captain and a crew of four, and an average catch was about two thousand head of salmon. Often they made three or four catches a day. When you figure this out on paper like we just did, you will find that three catches amounts to three thousand, three hundred and seventy-five dollars a day. This was divided six ways —one share to the boat, one to the captain who generally owned her, and one to each member of the crew. At six hundred and seventy-five dollars per man, per day, this ain't exactly chopped salmon! Now you take four or five hundred of these healthy young animals with two or three thousand bucks tucked in their jeans, in a small isolated town with no place to spend it and nothing to do except go from one saloon to another, and just mix this up with a movie company on location . . . and something's got to give. Well, we gave!

We found a sanctuary, seven miles outside of town along the narrow gravel road with the bay on one side and the piney woods on the other, deep in the wilderness and up a steep, narrow, rickety flight of board stairs. It was our haven. It looked like a summer cottage. Asbury Park Provincial! But this cottage was different. This cottage, to borrow a phrase from the Welsh, was the local "knocking shop!" Compared to the other spots this was the "Twenty One," the "Stork Club," and "Romanoffs" of Petersburg. All we ever saw of this establishment was the bar room, which looked like a rumpus room in a private house. It was a dimly-lit, medium-sized room with a small bar and three chromium and blue glass tables with red leatherette chairs. And, of course, the inevitable juke box. The place was run by three girls who doubled as bartenders and cocktail waitresses. These girls bore no resemblance whatever to "Klondike Kate" or "Diamond Lil." They looked like respectable, small-town matrons on their way to the supermarket, except that no self-respecting small-town matron would be caught dead wearing those early Ginger Rogers, billiard-green felt slack suits with bell-bottom trousers, plus multi-colored mukluks on their feet. Those outfits, which seemed to be their only garments, were topped off by aluminum curlers and pink hairnets. *When* they ever took their hair out of those curlers and for what occasion, we never found out.

The first time we went to the "knocking shop" I must say we were quite impressed. It had a quiet rural air, and after the din of the downtown saloons this was a welcome relief. There was only one other customer, a man named Mauldwin, seated on a stool at the end of the bar, quietly smoking his pipe, nursing his drink, and minding his own business. He was clad in a suit of long woolen underwear, complete with built-in feet and escape hatch. For a minute we thought he was doing a lingerie ad for *Field and Stream*. We found out later that he had been sitting on that same stool for three days and three nights quietly drinking. We learned that he was a captain, whose boat was in dry dock while he was in wet dock. We never once went to the "knocking shop" that Captain Mauldwin was not sitting on that same stool in his long johns, serenely guzzling. We wondered when he slept, if ever, and if so, where. One night our question was answered. Mauldwin gulped down his drink, got himself off the bar stool, reeled to the center of the room, reached behind a drape for a clothes line which caused a trap door to open in the beaver board ceiling, and a rope ladder to flop down. Then, hand over hand, he hauled himself up into the eaves to his boudoir, pulling his ladder behind him. After a little beauty nap, Mauldwin, completely refreshed, opened his little door, let down his ladder, and descended to his bar stool where he battened down his hatches and ordered a fresh drink which meant drinks for all.

They had a charming little house rule at the "knocking shop." There was no such thing as ordering a single drink. If you asked for a drink, automatically anyone who needed a refill—however slight—got a full one, too . . . on you. Thus, if the place was fairly full, your tab per compulsory round was about eighteen dollars, paid on the spot. Eight-

een bucks a slug was pretty steep even by Petersburg stand-
ards. This helped to keep out some of the riff-raff. Now,
mind you, we watched Mauldwin do his rope trick for ten
nights without ever once hearing the sound of his voice.
Then, suddenly, one night out of nowhere he stood up on his
stool and in a voice of thunder announced, "By the good
Lord Harry! Give me ten thousand men tried and true,
and I shall rule the world! I am ready to march and they
will follow! For I am their leader! Today all of Petersburg!
Tomorrow the world!!! Follow me for I am your leader
even though I am only a corporal!!!" After this rather sin-
ister announcement, Mauldwin raised his arm in salute
and slumped back to his perch. I remember thinking to
myself, "if this idiot starts hanging paper, we're all in
trouble."

Shortly after Mauldwin's announcement that he was
going to conquer the world, news came that his fishing
boat had been repaired and was ready to sail. Mauldwin
left that night after paying his bill which amounted to
$3,482 for his ten-day stay. We often wondered how
Mauldwin explained that little item on his income tax
report. Was it for "entertaining clients who ate an awful
lot of salmon?" or "rental of a penthouse apartment at the
height of the season?" or could it have been "expenses in-
curred while recruiting an army with which to conquer
the world?"

I remember one night having a drink with one of the
establishment's "cocktail waitresses." I asked this tacky
tart what she charged for her favors. She replied, "$500."
I was nonplussed, to say the least. I asked her how long
she stayed up in Alaska and she said, "Three months, the
length of the fishing season." I asked her what she was
going to do after that. I figured at $500 a pop, she would
be off to Eldorado in Palm Springs to play golf with Ike,

rent Onassis' yacht for a cruise of the Mediterranean, or join the Prince and her serene highness for a month of skiing in St. Moritz. Not at all. This drab courtesan informed me that at the conclusion of her present engagement, she was considering journeying to Hollywood to continue her professional career. I looked at her in amazement. I said,

"In Hollywood, for $500 . . . we get names!!!"

All in all, our forty-ninth state threw the "Ice Palace" company a curve. We went to Petersburg for the summer scenes because the weather in August was supposed to be clear and sunny, but for three solid weeks it never did anything but rain. Then we were due to go to Point Barrow, which is up near the North Pole, for some snow and blizzard scenes, but crocuses and daffodils appeared from nowhere. So, in the best Hollywood tradition, we returned to Burbank and shot our Alaska scenes where God intended Alaska to be in the first place . . . on the Warner Brothers back lot.

Shortly after my Alaska location I was in the lounge of a New York bound jet plane, when rough weather caused me to be strapped into a love seat with a typical Texan. He was wearing a stetson and boots and drinking "bubbin" and branch water. He was doing the usual Texas bragging, and among other things, he told me he owned thirty acres.

"Thirty acres," I exclaimed, "that's not so much for a Texan!"

"Downtown Dallas?" he retorted.

Then he proceeded to bore me with a long tale about how he and Lyndon and Glenn and Jake had just been on a safari, so to keep the ball rolling, I started telling him that I had just been to Alaska. I told him how high the mountains were, how large the salmon were, and how a friend of mine had made millions selling No-Cal blubber to the Eskimos and topped it by needling him with the fact that since its admission to the union, Alaska was now our largest state.

"Oh yeah?" he drawled, "Alaska bigger than Texas? Just wait till it melts."

4 ham on ham

EVERY BUSINESS has its status symbols. With the advertising man, it's his Jaguar, his membership in the right country club, and his split-level farmhouse on the corner of Cobblers Bench Lane and Cornwallis Ct. With the office worker, it's an invitation to the boss' house for dinner, a monogrammed bowling ball, and the key to the men's room. The frequenters of the Catskill mountain resorts have their status symbols too. It's best exemplified in the pride of the mothers in their sons' professions, like the middle-aged lady at one resort who ran up to the lifeguard screaming, "Help! Help! My son, the doctor, is drowning!!!"

Status symbols are subject to change. I can best explain this to you by quoting a speech I made at a banquet honoring Larry Sherry, the relief pitcher, who almost single-handedly won the pennant and the World Series for the Los Angeles Dodgers. Before I got up to speak, much had been made in jest by celebrities on the speakers' dais, of the fact that Mr. Sherry was Jewish, which left me the perfect opening for—

"Gentlemen, I'm very honored to be here at a banquet honoring Mr. Sherry. There have been numerous references tonight to the fact that this brilliant young athlete and his teammate, another great pitcher, Sandy Koufax, are of the Jewish faith. Before I came here tonight I did some research and found that down through the ages there had been many famous Jewish athletes—David with his sling shot—that professional strong man, Samson—and that Stone Age Eddie Arcaro, Ben Hur. But the most amazing thing I discovered was that even the Vikings were Jewish . . . TONY CURTIS! . . . KIRK DOUGLAS . . . !!!

(Laughter and applause.)

"However more important, these two young pitchers have raised the status of baseball to a high place in Jewish culture. Until this auspicious World Series, can you imagine what would have happened if a nice Jewish girl had come home to her family and announced that she was going to marry a second baseman? But now all this has changed! Why, just the other day at Grossingers, a distraught middle-aged lady ran up to the lifeguard screaming, 'Help! Help! My son, the utility outfielder, is drowning!!!' "

And so in our business we have our status symbols too—living on the right side of Sunset Blvd., giving a party with your garden encased in a giant tent plus a dance floor over the pool, and, if you are a man, being invited to play in the Bing Crosby tournament at Pebble Beach, and need I add—a summer in Europe, to say the least. But there are two more status symbols— having your house on "Person to Person," and being tapped for "This Is Your Life." Of these, the only one I found harrowing was being surprised on "This Is Your Life." Surprised? I was

astounded! Wherever I go people invariably ask me,
"Were you really surprised on 'This Is Your Life'? Come
on now . . . admit it!"

Again I reiterate I was completely bowled over!!! The
amazing thing about this is that Henny had known about
it for ten solid months and had kept her mouth shut. Come
to think of it . . . it just occurred to me . . . any woman
who can keep a secret that long is not to be trusted!!! How
about that, Henny?

O.K. Jimmy . . . now it can be told! It came about this
way. We had written our first book, *Rocks On The Roof.*
The manuscript was accepted for publication in January
of 1958, and the book was to be released on November
26th of the same year. We were in New York the week it
was accepted, and one morning the publisher called me
on the phone and asked me if I could come into the office
to see him that afternoon . . . alone! He made quite a
point out of my coming alone.

"Promise me you won't mention this to Jimmy," he said.

I have been an actress since I was a teen-ager and met
one or two on-the-make producers . . . but a sexy publisher? Not round and round that desk again!

When I arrived I was relieved to see our press agent,
Charles Pomerantz, sitting there too. The publisher welcomed me quite correctly. He ordered no calls for the
duration of the conference, locked the door, took a sip of
water, picked up my hand, looked deep into my eyes and
said,

"Henny, I want you to tell me the absolute truth. Do
you think you can keep a very important secret?" I in-
dignantly assured him that I was the best secret-keeper in
Hollywood and to hurry up and tell me!!

"Well," he whispered, "as you know we have a tentative
date of publication of your book for late October or early

November, and Charlie tells me that by coincidence Ralph Edwards wants to do Jimmy on 'This Is Your Life,' on or about the same time. Now, if we can tie the two together, this would be great publicity for the book."

I was horrified! "You can't!" I cried, "Jim lives in constant terror of that show. He won't even go downtown on a Wednesday. He won't go to a party if Ralph Edwards is going to be there! Not a chance!! Why, he said if I ever connive with Ralph Edwards, he'll cut his wrists, he'll divorce me—he'll melt my Charga-Plates!!!"

"But," said the publisher, "it's a guaranteed sale of 100,-000 books."

"Really?" I sang, "what night can we make it?"

"Well," said Charlie Pomerantz, "I've got a call in now to Ralph Edwards, and I'm waiting . . ."

"No," I told them, "not a chance. We'll never fool Jimmy. He's wise to that show. Every Wednesday night he hides under the bed. And anyway, we've booked passage at last. This summer our big dream is coming true! I haven't told you yet, Charlie, Jimmy and I are going to Europe!!! Isn't that great!$%!!"

"You can't!" they both wailed, "you can't leave now!!!"

"We have to!" I broke in with, "you see, now that he's an author, he wants to take a tramp steamer and just bum around Europe!"

"He won't have to take a tramp steamer," replied Charlie, "he can stay home and be a bum right here. Now listen to me, Henny, this is important. We need you here all summer to help us plan the show. It's a bigger job than you know. But one thing you don't know is this. Ralph Edwards is going to tape the show."

"So what?" I was confused.

"Simmer down . . . and let me explain, Henny. The show still goes on on Wednesday night at its regular time, but with tape, Ralph can surprise his subjects any day or night of the week. He can surprise Jim in his dressing room at the studio, on the golf course, in a barber shop . . . anywhere! How they'll trap him, you and I will have to figure out. But believe me . . . it *can* be done. Now remember, honey, the important thing is we all have to keep this a dead secret. If Ralph finds out that Jimmy even suspects, he'll call off the whole thing, even at the last minute . . . even if he has to play a rerun! Now remember, we're in this together. There is no turning back. The die is cast! And one last thing . . . KEEP YOUR BIG FAT MOUTH SHUT!!!" We sealed the bargain with bone-dry Martinis.

Now followed a series of events that would rival anything in the files of Interpol. Jimmy did everything to blow the candy store. First of all, I encouraged him to play golf every day. I begged him to play on weekends, holidays, our anniversary . . . anytime at all. I urged him to play poker with the boys nightly. Now, all of a sudden he didn't want to play golf! Poker bored him! All he wanted to do was stay home and neck!!

Ralph Edwards assigned a girl executive of "This Is Your Life," named Jan Boehm to me. I told Jimmy I had a new girl friend named Jan whom I had met in the beauty parlor. If Jim was home when she called, we talked girl talk, and through our feminine code decided where and when to meet. If he was out, she came flying over and we talked about Jim's life and the people who had played a part in it. We sorted all those old pictures they use on that show, and, with Charlie Pomerantz' help and close co-operation, we dreamed up two life plots with two separate sets of characters. The reason for this is that if one or two key characters in the first script were not available for the time the show was set to be taped, we could eliminate that whole idea and use the second one.

I must explain that we didn't actually write the script.

We simply outlined it and then it was given to Mort Lewis of the Ralph Edwards staff who whipped it into proper "This Is Your Life" style, and gave it its approximate timing. The speeches were written for everyone but Jimmy. I could sort of indicate what they might be and how I thought he would react to the given situation, thanks to my knowing Jimmy so well. (NOTE TO WIVES: It is interesting and rather surprising to see how close I came.)

On November 2nd, Jim and I were doing a television show. I got a phone call at rehearsal, where they didn't encourage such things, ordering me to go to the Ladies Room on the Main Floor as soon as I could break away. This was a pretty odd request and rather hard to do, since for some reason Jimmy insisted on walking me clear to the door. In there waited Jan Boehm.

"All right," said Jan, "today is Sunday. D-Day is next Friday at 5:30. The first rehearsal is tomorrow at 1:00 in Ralph's office. Do you think you can lose Jimmy and be there?"

Although I didn't know how I was going to do that, I assured her that she had nothing to worry about and she could count on me.

"Oh, and by the way," I added, "which script are we going to do and with which people?"

"Well," said Jan, "we couldn't get hold of Victor Mature. He's in Italy shooting a picture. We couldn't get Keenan Wynn. He's in Florida making *Hole In The Head,* and the director wouldn't let him go. We can't get David Wayne. He's still playing on Broadway in *Say Darling,* and unfortunately, it's a hit. Bill Feather, the Cleveland publisher, whom Jimmy roomed with in prep school, is out of the country, and the golf foursome of Donald O'Connor, Joe Kirkwood, Jr. and Jimmy Demaret was ruined because Donald is televising a spectacular on the same night. So this is the other script. Now what do you want me to do with it?"

"Here are the keys to my car," I told her. "Drive out to our house while Jim and I do this show. Put the script in my make-up kit in the trunk, and then hide the keys in the ash-tray. Jim never touches my car . . . so it's perfectly safe."

That night, as against any unforeseen emergencies, I waited till Jimmy was sound asleep, then quietly tiptoed out of the house and loaded my car trunk. I put in it my make-up kit with the script hidden on the bottom under my cosmetics. In a plastic bag I had my waist cinch, panties, stockings, shoes, jewelry to be worn and my beautiful new dress I had had made for the show. It was a Count Sarmi—black organza with a simple bodice, tiny sleeves, and a daringly short skirt made of deep flounces which contained fifty-two yards of fabric in the skirt alone and stood way out all around. All I wore with it was a string of pearls, pearl earrings and my engagement and wedding rings. This dress was such a smash that I am still getting fan letters from women who want to know if I'll give it to them, sell it to them, or let them make copies. I still wear it from time to time and soon I am going to give it to the Costume Institute. That night I also had the good sense to take a flashlight with me and when, as I dreaded, Jim woke up and came out, I pretended that I must have lost my earring and was busily looking around under the car with my big police flashlight. He never suspected a thing. He also never suspected a thing when on Friday morning—"This Is Your Life" showday—his car broke down and he had to borrow mine without telling me. He never opened the trunk, thank heavens, while I and the whole Ralph Edwards staff, to whom I shriekingly related this on the phone, shuddered as we waited for him to return it.

When I reported for the first rehearsal, there was Axel Gruenberg to direct us. It was the first time I had seen Ax since the many times we had worked for him in radio some years back. The entire cast of Jim's family and old friends were there with the exception of Jim's mother. For security reasons, she, who was to be the big surprise of the evening, was being flown in right before the show, kept in a dressing room—not even to appear backstage during the performance—and brought out right before her entrance just before the end of the whole thing. Not even I knew anything about it as they wanted an honest emotional reaction from both of us. I suspected nothing. They told me her doctor had advised against the trip and I believed them, as she had been quite ill. The shock and thrill of seeing her walking toward us, looking her most beautiful, proved to be the high point of the entire production.

That first rehearsal day I met many old friends I had known before, and also Janet Moss with whom Jim went to kindergarten, and Colonel Charles B. Richmond, the president of Kentucky Military Institute in Louisville, Kentucky, about whom I had heard so much. This was the school that Jim and Victor Mature attended together and about whom we wrote in *Rocks On The Roof* in the chapter called "The Old Vic," as follows:

> This is Jimmy speaking: Because I have worked with just about every star in the business, civilians (people not in our trade) invariably ask me who is actually the most colorful character in Hollywood. I never fail to floor them with my answer—Victor Mature. To us, Victor Mature is the most colorful and also one of the funniest people in Hollywood.
>
> I first came in contact with Vic when I was a kid. We both reluctantly attended Kentucky Military Institute

just outside of Louisville, which incidentally is Vic's
home town. This is a very fine disciplinary institute of
learning, but to Vic and me, it was Alcatraz with tui-
tion. We were thrown together a lot in school because
we repeatedly drew the same punishments. Our two
most common offenses were the unmilitary state of
our rooms and our persons. We were each known as
"Cadet Slob."

The boys who behaved and obeyed the rules were
allowed to go into town every Monday. In the years
Vic and I went to K. M. I., we never once made it.
We made up for it, however, by giving gay, illegal
cocktail parties in our quarters. This being prohibition, we served a delightful and very potent drink.
Lemon soda and Aqua Velva. Our bar was a hole
under a loose board in the floor.

One day we were on the brink of expulsion and were
called up before the Colonel. Vic, when cornered by
the authorities, had a way of infuriating them even
further by becoming excessively military. He would
click his heels, salute every word and agree with
every charge hurled at him. When the Colonel threw
a thunderbolt at him like, "You are the worst cadet
in the hundred-year history of this academy," without taking a beat, Vic would click his heels, salute a
shade too smartly and answer, "Yes, sir!" salute and
click) "You're absolutely right, sir!" (more saluting
and clicking). "I agree with you one hundred per-
cent, sir!" (windmill of salutes and clicks).

By now, the Colonel was enraged. "Cadet Mature," he
shouted, "I'm never wrong about one of my cadets,
and I predict you will wind up in the gutter, a bum!
You're guilty of insubordination, your quarters are a
disgrace, and you're constantly out of uniform! Why,
you wouldn't last five minutes at the Point!! With this
disgraceful record, what actually are your plans when
you get out of here?"

"Sir," said Mature eagerly, with great clicking and saluting, "I'm going to Hollywood and become a movie star."

This was too much for the Colonel. Smoke came out of his ears as he yelled, "Get out!—Be a movie star! Never heard of anything so ridiculous. I suppose you're going with him, Backus. Well, get out! Get out both of you! And as long as you're in this academy, and I'm sure that won't be too long, stay out of my sight! Just stay out of my sight, both of you!! Get out!!!"

Twenty years later, Vic and I were reunited for the first time. He hadn't changed a bit. He looked exactly the same as he had at fourteen. We were making a picture called "Interference" at RKO Studios, and we got to reminiscing about our days at dear old K. M. I. Suddenly, Vic got an idea. The set we were working in was a beautiful Park Avenue penthouse. He called over two scantily clad starlets, got the prop man to give us four glasses and a magnum of champagne. We filled the glasses, put the starlets on our laps and asked the still-man to shoot a picture of us. The picture turned out perfectly, and Vic sent it off to the Colonel with an appropriate autograph:

> Best wishes from Cadets Mature and Backus.
> P.S. What are your honor students doing?

Well, that's what we said about Vic in our first book. Jim told it to me and I believed every word of it! I fell in love with the lovable Colonel at first rehearsal, but he disillusioned me completely when he told me that both boys were terrible liars and . . . model students!!

We rehearsed for a few hours on Monday, Tuesday, Wednesday, Thursday, and then of course there was Friday. The guests had been contacted starting on the Friday before the show and housed at the Hollywood Roosevelt Hotel where Ralph also gave the after-show parties. On Friday, Jim was told that he and I were both to be at the Pickwick Book Shop at 5:30 (one of our town's largest and most popular book stores) to autograph books, give out some interviews, and pose for pictures, as this was the official day of the debut of *Rocks On The Roof* . . . and this was to be our launching. Jim thought that all this was really what was going to happen on Friday, November 7th. He expected me to drive down with him, as we always went places together, with Jim in the driver's seat. But again, I lied rather well. I told him that I was having a new dress made at a new dressmaker's and I wanted to wear it for the newsreels and it would not be finished till five, and, since the so-called dressmaker lived near the Pickwick Bookshop, I would change there and she would drive me over. He swallowed it all including the mythical newsreels that I added to give it some extra pizzazz.

By pre-arrangement, just as I was leaving for the dress rehearsal at N.B.C.'s Television City in Burbank, never to return till the show was over, Charlie Pomerantz dropped in with a lot of exciting lies about added interviews at the bookshop and frothy mélange of fibs calculated to keep Jim nicely grounded until time to dress and go. One of Charlie's main functions was to get Jim to the store on time. Also the N.B.C. truck housing the T.V. equipment was on a side street beside "Pickwick," so Charlie somehow had to talk Jim out of driving by any route that included that particular street. Charlie had his work cut out . . . and he did it magnificently!

Now, here is the way it all worked, and, I might add, without one single hitch.

HENNY'S SCHEDULE

12:00 noon	Left home
12:30	Checked into N.B.C. Undressed. Got in robe. Had hair washed and set.

1:00	Had run-through with rest of cast.
2:00	Went back to dressing room. Had make-up put on. Had hair combed out. Hair sprayed with lacquer. Got into show clothes.
4:00	Entire cast did dress rehearsal with some attempt made to approximate what Jim would say and with what pace for final try at timing. (This rehearsal included the flashing of the many photographs I had loaned them on to the screen for the first time.)
5:00	Was locked into dressing room until show time. Assumed that this was normal "This Is Your Life" procedure and didn't question it. (Their reason for locking me in, however, was because my mother-in-law, Daisy, was due to arrive and they were afraid to risk a chance meeting in the hall.)
5:25	Was led out to backstage area and parked there. (We had a monitor back there so that we could watch the show on T.V. and get ready with the aid of the screen to make our entrances.)
5:30	A tense moment. Ralph would now discover Jim at Pickwick. He did! Was better than anticipated! Jim was positively stunned!!!
5:35	The tape is stopped till arrival of Jim from bookshop. We sit and wait.
6:00	Arrive with Jim . . . and show goes on!

JIMMY'S SCHEDULE

12:00 noon	Awakened by maid. Informed Mr. Pomerantz downstairs. Was furious. What kind of nonsense is this? Waking man in middle of night!
12:05	Charlie Pomerantz enters bedroom. Encourages

me to breakfast, dress and shave. Talking all the time.

3:04   Interminable brunch with Mr. P. Three hours discussing matters that could be settled in ten minutes. What a bore!

4:00   Sitting, staring. Mr. P. still talking, grinning, making no sense. Could be—drunk? Or in need psychiatric care??

4:05   Trying to go to men's room . . . privately.

4:10   No luck!

4:15   Bob Williams from Philadelphia Bulletin shows up to interview me before autograph party. Am grounded!!!

4:30   Charlie Pomerantz decided gray suit not photogenic. Go upstairs. Makes me try on entire wardrobe. Settles on dark blue suit. Could he be homosexual???

5:00   Big fight with Charlie who insists on doing driving as Bob still interviewing me. Could be Charlie nervously maladjusted???

5:18   More words with Pomerantz as he drives by cockamamie route. Make mental note. Get new press agent!

5:25   Arrive Pickwick. Practically no one there. Autographing what? For whom?

5:28   No Henny! Never known to be late!! Worried!!!

5:30   Ralph Edwards, old friend, comes in to store. Stupid idiot! Carrying microphone and huge light. Misses point of my autograph party. Hands me a book of his to autograph. Mumbles something about this being my life—felt like giving him rap on—Oh, my God!!! Oh no!!! Couldn't be!!**$%¢!

"THIS IS YOUR LIFE" . . . JIM BACKUS!!!

I've been ambushed!$%¢%¢!

Well, Henny fooled me all right, but it was worth it. My mother looked beautiful and had the thrill of her life on "This Is Your Life." The after-show party got off to a running start, it being Friday, and kind of slopped over Saturday and Sunday with Bloody Marys and reminiscences at our house. Then it sort of oozed over Monday with a hungover guided tour. Then on Tuesday, the men played golf while the women had lunch at Romanoffs and went through Saks Fifth Avenue like a plague of locusts. Since none of the guests had ever met each other before, but had suddenly become fast friends, having been welded together by booze and sentiment, this called for a number of farewell fêtes as they dribbled off homeward—all expenses paid! If the ladies and gentlemen from out of my past had stayed much longer, they could have done another "This Is Your Life" on this "This Is Your Life."

Selfishly speaking, one of the nicest things about that show was the gifts they gave us. It's nice to have a young man going through dramatic school on your scholarship. When he's a big star he can give me small parts in his pictures—sort of an emotional annuity for my old age. Then there was the motion picture camera and projector. Of course, I had to send Henny to Rochester to learn how to work them. They also gave us a color T.V. set. The fellow who adjusted it must have been queer for blue— everything came out looking like a set of dishes. This was not the fault of the set, however. I can't work anything. I once tried to repair one of our early television sets and got the wires crossed with the vacuum cleaner, and John Cameron Swayze came on and sucked the wallpaper off the wall and the petals from his carnation flew all over the room. Now, about the charm bracelet with its thirty-six giant jeweled charms. My wife is not exactly serene. She's given to a great many broad gestures, and the noise from the bracelet is deafening. The first time she wore it, when I came home I thought she was making love to a Good Humor man.

"Person to Person" is almost as harrowing as "This Is Your Life," but in a completely different way. At least you are prepared for it. Once the Jovian thunderbolt is hurled at you from the heights of Madison Avenue, a carefully prepared chain of events takes place. First of all there is the correspondence, with the producer, who comes out in person to check over your house and have a little private talk with both of you. The producer, with the musical sounding name of Perry Lafferty, came out, looked over the house, made mental notes on where the cables would come in, where the sound truck would go and where to put the field kitchen to feed the giant crew. Could they dolly the camera up the staircase without taking off the bannister? Would the police cooperate in clearing our section of the street? Would we mind having our phone service disrupted for twelve hours? Then he told us that the only time they could tape this was the second week in December.

He was no sooner out of the house when Henny sent up a barrage of feminine objections. December? That was the time I had promised her Christmas in Paris! I assured her that we would go in March for her birthday! Then she got nervous about Edward R. Murrow getting cigarette ashes all over everything. I countered that one with the fact that Edward R. Murrow was no longer doing the show—it was now Charles Collingwood.

"What about those cables," she moaned, "and all those men tramping all over the place?" I cooled her with, "It didn't seem to bother Pat Nixon! And there's a housewife scheduled the week before us named Jacqueline Kennedy, who hasn't objected too strenuously!"

After I managed to get her objections overruled, it was my turn to regret it. She ordered new draperies that budgetwise weren't earmarked till June! Then because the opening shot was in the garden, she had it re-landscaped. This in mid-December! Then she had to get blue uniforms for our maids, Essie and Willa, as neither black nor white photograph well. The phrase, "We have to get the house looking pretty for Mr. Collingwood," became a battle cry. Then she went into deep consultation with Don Loper. She had her orders from Mr. Lafferty. Since ours is a formal house and we were to be going to a party after they finished shooting, mention of which was to be injected into the script, he asked her to wear a party dress. It could not be white. It could not be black. It could not be bare. It must have a full skirt for the batteries that would have to be attached to her thighs, so that she would not have any visible wires. The neckline had to be cut so that the microphone hidden there would not show.

In early November, the following letter arrived:

Mr. and Mrs. Jim Backus,
Bel Air, California

Dear Jim and Henny:

This is to confirm that we shall do a script and technical survey with you for PERSON TO PERSON on Sunday, December 4, from 4:30-6:30 P.M.

We will plan to shoot the spot the afternoon of Saturday, December 10.

I know that we will be in touch long before this, but just put this in the book, because we have a pretty heavy schedule and need to finalize things as far in advance as possible.

Best personal wishes,
PERRY LAFFERTY

They did their script conference with us and their technical survey, all of which took exactly the amount of time the letter said it would. We found our Mr. Lafferty ran a tight ship.

In late November we received this letter.

CBS TELEVISION NETWORK

Television City,
Hollywood, California

Mr. and Mrs. Jim Backus
Bel Air, California

Dear Jim and Henny:

This is to confirm that our director, Bob Dailey, and our writer, David Moore, will drop by next Sunday, December 4th at 4:30 to talk with you about the content of your spot for "PERSON TO PERSON." This meeting will take about two hours.

We will plan to shoot the spot beginning at 2:00 P.M. on Friday, December 9th. This will take three to four hours. The technicians will arrive for setup about 9:00 A.M.

Mr. Dailey and Mr. Moore are in residence at the Bel Air Hotel, and you should check with them if you have any problems.

I know that this letter seems formal, but you will understand that my basic squaredom comes out in Lotus Land.

Best wishes,

PERRY LAFFERTY, Producer
cc: Messrs.   Collingwood, PERSON TO PERSON
              Dailey, Moore,
              Miss Jan Murray

This meeting again took exactly the length of time Mr. Lafferty said it would.

At this meeting Perry Lafferty told us that the make-up man would be there to make Henny up at 11:00 A.M.

and that she could choose her hairdresser. She chose her favorite, Ginny Darcy, one of the best in our business. It was Ginny who went to Monaco with Grace Kelly to design her coiffeur for the wedding. She still goes back and forth to do her hair for special occasions. In Henny's case, only her serene highness and her hairdresser know!

Since my make-up job consists of a once-over lightly with a sponge, to obliterate my heavy beard, they let me sleep till noon. Henny was the first one up, so I'll let her tell you about it.

This is Henny . . . and the shock of what I saw left me numb! I got up at about 10:30 and looked out of my front window. Although there wasn't a sound to be heard, there were men swarming all over the driveway. A huge mobile unit which was actually a combination sound truck and tape projection truck, and was about double the size of a moving van, was parked there. The men were tiptoeing all about with lights, cables, and all sorts of equipment. I put on a robe and crept out of my room. I could hear the Lord of the manor snoring in his lair. Nothing bothers him! From my room, since they hadn't gotten in there yet, on down the hall and the stairs there were dropcloths. Huge arc lights studded the way. I managed to get downstairs. There were more people in our house than I ever dreamed it could hold . . . men checking things out with each other, smoking, drinking coffee, drinking cokes, having whispered consultations, script girls and secretaries receiving hush hush orders. I'll say this for them—they didn't make a sound all morning. We never even heard that mob arrive!

I went into the living room. The place was a shambles!! There were big thick cables snaking their way through every window. There was all sorts of lighting equipment; a T.V. monitor stood in a corner; a young man with earphones was whispering into a talkback; all my beautiful tall graceful flower arrangements that I had stayed up to do the night before were replaced with low ones. Mine would obscure us, I was told—and they had moved my furniture all around! Better grouping for their camera angles, I was informed.

I went into the dining room. There were more of same. And seated on my high kitchen stool which they had draped with a velvet cloth, was Charles Collingwood. Behind him was a false wall. This is sort of a screen arrangement that they carry with them. It is a copy of the wall on the set they use back in the studio in New York. He had a monitor so that he could see us and get his cues and we had one in each room they were to photograph. There was a talkback arrangement, too, which wasn't always clear and caused a lot of retakes. A phone call to a satellite would have been clearer. Perry was in the dining room, too, going over the script with Mr. Collingwood, who was charming. I must have looked pretty stricken, for Mr. Lafferty assured me again that half an hour after they wrapped up the tape our house would be back in perfect order. I couldn't believe it. Maybe the house . . . but what about the garden? How could they run cables in every window without trampling the flowers? I refrained from making mention of this. It was show day! Time to go to work! Relax and enjoy it, I told myself! One cup of coffee and up to make-up and hair!

At noon that was over and it was time to wake Jimmy for his cold sponge, and oh yes . . . time for someone to strap those batteries on me. I had forgotten about that in all the excitement. Ginny told me that they couldn't tape them on until I was actually in my dress. So I got into my gown and some kind soul brought my spouse a cup of coffee so he would wake up gently.

I was brought up in show business where everyone is

hardened to performers running around backstage scantily clad, making quick changes in the wings or being dressed on stage in slight attire, so I felt nothing at being strapped into those two batteries. However, I couldn't help but wonder. What about some of the dignified older ladies who went through this same procedure. Just think of some of the women who have been on "Person to Person." Just remember one thing—once the batteries are strapped on, every single sound you make, no matter how faint, can be heard in the sound track and you'd better watch it because, believe me, YOU . . . ARE . . . BROADCAST-ING!!!

It was show time . . . I mean tape time . . . and we followed the script which all three of us, Jim, Mr. Collingwood and I had learned in sequence. I was happy it was tape time and not live show time because once, not too long ago, we had rented a town house on upper Fifth Avenue, and while we were living there I was called to California while Jim remained in the East. At that time a very popular live program called "Wide Wide World," which was on Sunday afternoons, was doing a segment devoted to Fifth Avenue. I was sitting in the den of our California home watching this when I was pleased to see the camera panning to the house we were renting. Suddenly the announcer said, "This is one of the last of the classical townhouses. Let's examine it more closely."

With that the camera zoomed to the second story where the front French windows came clear to the floor. It was summer, and they were wide open. Much to my horror, standing there framed in one of the windows was my loving husband who had undoubtedly just gotten up. His sole garb was a pair of sagging pajama bottoms. He was busily doing his early morning scratching. With my eyes glued to the set I leapt to the telephone. Long distance did a record job. In a twinkling I had him! "Doll," I yelled, "get away from that window! Stop scratching yourself! You're on 'Wide Wide World!!!'" You might say Jimmy started in television from scratch.

We began shooting early . . . at 1:00 P.M. It took until six to complete the script. When we got finished the place was more of a shambles than ever, but we didn't mind. Everybody liked what they had seen in the sound truck. They were able to see each segment immediately after it was taped to check it for flaws—technical or otherwise. And after we were through they ran the whole tape for us. It was amazing! We had just finished . . . and here we were watching it. It was magic! What we saw took about half an hour. They could cut out what they chose.

To celebrate we invited everybody back into the house for a drink! Now, this was pretty hard to believe, but the house was spotless! It shone! I wasn't there to watch them so I don't know how they did it! It was just exactly like it was the night before! Cleaner, maybe!

"Come outside and check your garden," said Perry. I did. Not a blade of grass was bruised. Really, it was an astonishing thing.

"If you find later that any damage whatsoever has been done, please let us know and we will make good," Mr. Lafferty told me.

To this day we never found a single thing to complain about.

WARNING!

To those of you who have been stuck at other people's houses looking at their home movies!

Jim not only shows the prints they gave us of "This Is Your Life" and "Person to Person," but the home movies he took of them taking us—sort of white on white or ham on ham!—if you get what I mean!!!

STANTON KEENEY

5 going fishing with the game warden

This Is Henny——

Next to marital bliss and golf (which, believe me, is a photo finish), my husband loves parties. I kept wishing he'd love a party in Europe for a change! But he loves all kinds of parties—cocktail parties, clam bakes, cotillions, cookouts, bal masques, and barbecues. He's even been known to be the surprise guest at a baby shower. If he'd been born a girl, he would have spent most of his life leaping out of pies.

He loves to give parties too, especially barbecues. His steaks are very good. And why not? For charcoal he uses the steaks he barbecued the night before. I love to hear our guests thanking him for the wonderful dinner he cooked while I stand at the sink doing the dishes after having whipped up the dip, marinated the steaks, made the salad, lyonnaised the potatoes, buttered the home-baked rolls, and whipped the cream for the ice-box cake that I made the day before. I don't mind, hours later, having to go outdoors to put out the fire while he is sound asleep in bed still wearing his chef's cap. There is so much smoke from one of his banked fires that for days we keep getting messages from friendly Indians in Albuquerque.

Once on a particularly hot night, we were going to have a party after the theater, so I decided to give my guests a cold supper on the terrace. Instead of the inevitable indigestible Welsh Rarebit, I settled on a cold meat mold. This, with all the appropriate accompaniments and garnishes, would be sure to cause talk in the Betty Crocker circles. I added spices, cooked cereal, gelatin, and little surprises to finely chopped cooked meats. I'd show these grapefruits (affectionate term for native Californians) what graceful living was all about.

I oiled an oblong mold, poured in my mixture, and proudly put it in the refrigerator till we got back from the performance. It was a stimulating evening at the theater. When we returned home I went into the kitchen to assemble the dinner I'd prepared. I unmolded my cold meat! It was there that Jimmy found me in tears.

"Baby," he soothed, "what's the matter?"

"I made Spam!!!" I howled, pointing in horror.

Shortly after the Donald O'Connors came back from a six-month location in Rome for a picture called *Aladdin,* they bought the Joan Crawford house. (In Hollywood almost every home is known by a celebrated former owner's name rather than its address, like the "Garbo" house, the "Joe Schenck" house, the "Connie Bennett" house etc.) I could hardly wait to call Gloria and find out all about the trip and get some advice: what to pack, where to go, where to live, where to get my hair done and where to shop, among other things. After we exchanged pleasantries, Gloria suggested we have dinner with them that very night.

"Listen, Henny," she said, "While the boys are playing golf this afternoon, why don't you come over early and swim with me and I'll tell you all about the trip and answer all your questions. I'll even get you our suite from the manager of the Ritz in Paris. I'll write him a note for you. You'll love our suite. You can look out of the window and see Elizabeth Arden's on one side and Cartier's on the other! Please come. Only don't dress. It's just us . . . and we'll have a simple little pick-up supper."

I was delighted! We both love the O'Conners, and anyway I was dying to see the Crawford house that I had read so much about since my movie magazine days. It's a lovely, large, graceful house with plenty of room for the growing O'Connor family. Its grounds are enchanting and, in addition to an outside playroom with cabanas, there is also a real movie theater—not just a projection room, but an honest-to-goodness movie theater with wide screen, cinemascope and stereophonic sound. Between screenings, the chairs which fold are stored and Donald uses it as his rehearsal hall. The house has three drawing rooms —all magnificently furnished. The rugs are so thick that according to Donald, sometimes a hat goes across the room and they never know who's under it till it reaches the tile floor in the hall. This house is completely air conditioned. I know lots of houses are air conditioned—but on the outside?

My favorite room in the O'Connor manse is the dining room—a beautifully proportioned, elegant, completely authentic eighteenth century English room. Even the wall panels and the lighting fixtures are really of the period, to say nothing of the highly polished mahogany furniture with its long and lovely table that seats thirty-six. It was here that the four of us, barefooted and in terry cloth robes, sat down to the O'Connors' first formal dinner party in their new home. In our poolside garb we dined on caviar, champagne, pheasant and Crêpes Suzettes. With the brandy, Jim rose. He said,

"I'd like to propose a toast to our host and hostess and wish them all the health and happiness in the world in their new home. Donald is a very lucky man—lucky to have such a lovely wife—lucky to have such fine children —lucky to live in this road company San Simeon. Yes, Donald, you are a very lucky fellow. Even today on the golf course you were lucky. You made less than a hole in one. You missed the ball and sank the divot!"

Jim sat down to deafening recorded applause. This house really had everything! Then it was Donald's turn to speak.

"Thank you, Jimmy. Like you said, I am indeed a very lucky man. I am particularly lucky tonight because this is our wedding anniversary."

I looked at Jimmy in surprise. What were we doing here in this magnificent dining room looking like four beach bums on a special night like this.

Donald continued, "So, in honor of this great occasion, I've asked some people over to celebrate."

The French doors opened and a most distinguished man in full dress entered. He bowed slightly and then two more males in tails came in to be followed by three more. Then another one came in dressed just as formally as the six already in the room. All these strange and handsome men! Who were they? Gloria and I looked at each other in panic. Our hair was still wet and we didn't even have any lipstick on. What was going on? In came another group of formally attired gentlemen. And then some more! And still they came!! Would they never stop?

Suddenly they all clicked their heels together, bowed formally and left the room—and just a few seconds later from the drawing room came the strains of "The Anniversary Waltz," played on thirty-six violins. What a charm-

ing and romantic way to serenade your wife! The best
Jimmy ever did was three drunken caddies who played
on tissue paper and combs. Anyway, we danced till dawn.
It looked like a remake of "Mayerling."

On the way home I said, "You've got to admit it, Jimmy,
Donald is a thoughtful husband, but where in the world
did he get thirty-six violinists—and all so handsome! What
did he do, call up Zsa Zsa and ask her to send over some
of her rejects?"

"What do you mean, where did Donald get thirty-six
violinists," answered Jimmy. "From the union . . . where
else? I worked with most of those guys . . . and let me
tell you something, the leader is a very wealthy gypsy.
He owns a chain of empty stores."

This was one of the most unusual parties we ever went
to. It was the only one where the band outnumbered the
guests.

A more usual party with a rather novel ending was a
masquerade we attended a few years ago. A friend took
over a well-known restaurant in our town and gave a really
lavish ball. We couldn't think of what to wear until almost
the last minute when Jimmy got a brainstorm. Why not
the God Bacchus and Mrs. Bacchus? He quietly called
MGM, where he was making a picture at the time, and
asked the Wardrobe Department to send over what we
would require. They were wonderful! They sent me a
long white silk Grecian gown, gold sandals, gold hair
bands and gold jewelry of the period. The whole thing
was perfect and I loved it. They sent Jimmy gold sandals,
gold vine leaves for his hair which I curled on an iron,
gold hoop earrings and a short white toga. There was only
one thing; they forgot to send Bacchanalian lingerie!
When he bent over, more than his grape leaves were
showing. He tried wearing a pair of his own shorts, but
they came at least two inches below the hemline of his
toga. Pretty anachronous, to say the least! What to do

now? The situation was saved by our then maid, Mary who, having overheard our dilemma came in with the solution in her hand.

"Mr. Backus," she said, "I got jest the thing you need . . . and they gonna fit you fine! I bought me some new panties today, and in honor of this here occasion, I'm jest gonna give you one pair to wear under your little dress."

She handed him a brand new pair of peach-colored rayon pants with an elastic waistband. Jimmy couldn't have received a nicer present. He was delighted with his Lane Bryant jockey shorts. They saved the evening!

The costumes were dazzling! The ball was great fun and went on until the wee hours. All of the members of the movie colony were there . . . and so were the fan magazine photographers. They were out in full force, swarming all over us. Toward the end of the festivities, Jim spotted some friends at a table near the door. As he bent over to say a few words, the elastic waist-band on his panties broke and they slithered to the floor just as the photographers' flash bulbs went off. He bunched his toga about him, and with the panties still around his ankles, took four giant kangaroo leaps to the "Gentlemens." To this day they have never figured out what a pair of peach-colored panties were doing in the second stall from the right in the men's room at "Ciro's."

Subsequently, we attended two fabulous and quite contrasting parties—one in Dallas and one in Chicago. The Chicago party was given by Hugh Hefner, publisher of *Playboy* and owner of the "Playboy" clubs, at his incredible house.

Mr. Hefner is a rather remarkable gentleman who has created his giant empire (magazines, night clubs, products, etc.) while still in his early thirties. He is a lean young man who looks like a professor and whose life on the screen is being played by Tony Curtis. Which reminds me—when our first book *Rocks On The Roof* was to be made into a movie, the producer, Joe Pasternak, asked me who I felt should play Jim and me. After they ruled us out for being too much the type, I suggested Jack Lemmon for Jim and Doris Day, no less, for me. I'll bet if they asked Jim that question he would have screamed the place down until they agreed to allow him to play himself—and for the part of Henny—Brigitte Bardot! Fat chance!!!

The "Playboy" Clubs, as every businessman in the country now knows, originated with the one in Chicago. Since Jimmy was playing in a night club in that city, he was invited to make the "Playboy" his second home. Little did they know he'd bring me!—every time!!—I think!!! A wife at the "Playboy" club is about as welcome as a hernia at a weight lifters convention.

The Chicago club is in what was once a private town house. When you enter the building, you are confronted by a circular staircase which leads to one of the many bars. Little do you know that from the moment you appear in the doorway until you are seated at your table you are appearing on all the T.V. screens in every room of the club via closed circuit television—thanks to their carefully hidden camera. This is the second most popular amusement at the "Playboy!" The main feature of this place is the fact that your waitress is a beautiful young lady in mesh stockings, a gussied up waist cinch, long white ears, a little white fur tail—and that's all!! When our waitress seated us she said to Jimmy,

"My name is Karen . . . and I'm your bunny." His bunny? Well!!! Why don't they have a club for us girls where a guy in a loin cloth and muscles says,

"My name is Michael . . . and I'm your wolf!" I was so mad at this point I would have settled for Uncle Wiggly.

Since Chicago is the city of conventions, most of the men who frequent this club are from out of town and needless to say, they want to take the bunnies back to their hutch. So these girls, most of whom have been *Playboy's* "Playgirl of the Month," are provided with a manual which teaches them at least a dozen polite but firm ways of saying "NO." They are even warned that shills may be in the club to check on them. I suggested a sign for their dressing room: "Big Bunny Is Watching You." I don't know why they have bunnies for waitresses anyway. It must bollux up their bookkeeping. Everyone knows rabbits can't add—they just multiply!

Hugh Hefner gives a party every other Friday night, after his "Playboy" club closes, at his utterly amazing house. This astonishing mansion, which is down the street from the Ambassador, once belonged to an old distinguished Chicago family. That family would have a hard time recognizing it today. The facade has not been touched. But the interior!!! The house is one conversation piece after another! First of all there is a ramp which goes around in back of the house and up to a garage which opens off Mr. Hefner's bedroom, where he can park his Maserati, Jaguar, Mercedes-Benz, or whatever car he happens to be driving. I guess he must belong to the "Car Of The Month" club.

In several of the rooms, all of which seem to be on different levels, if you're too fatigued to use the stairs, there's a handy firemen's pole on which you can slide down to the next bar. My favorite room was the one on the lowest level next to the foam-rubber grotto. This one had black velvet papered walls and was pitch black, with the exception of the illuminated color transparencies of the "Playgirls Of The Month" in their original poses or improvements thereof. On one wall was a pane of glass through which you could watch the swimmers in the indoor pool. The pool had a waterfall and behind that the celebrated foam-rubber grotto, which, if you were a sturgeon would be a great place to deposit some roe. Adjoining the pool was a fully equipped steam room and gym. There were so many guests at these parties, it was the sole function of one maid to assign cabanas and hand out bathing suits and towels.

The purpose of the parties is to entertain the actors performing in Chicago after they are finished with their own shows. So officially they start at 2:00 A.M. There is a uniformed guard at the door to see that there are no crashers. An attendance of three or four hundred invited guests plus the "Playboy" bunnies and their "cotton-tail" friends is not unusual. There was a mélange of visiting Hollywood and Broadway celebrities, international playboys, the entire staff of Mr. Hefner's magazines, plus a few contributors, a handful of backers, every current nightclub act in Chicago, and the roster of visiting baseball teams, which in my naiveté I thought went beddy-bye at 10 o'clock. The men all looked perfectly correct in their dark suits, but I was completely fascinated by the attire of the girls. They wore anything! Evening gowns, street clothes, shorts, pedal pushers and even a smattering of bathing suits. All of the great jazz musicians in Chicago were there—with instruments. But for us the floor show was the guests! We had to leave early though—6:00 A.M.

The next day we were having brunch on the roof of the Ambassador-East, where we were staying, when we heard a din from the street twenty floors below. We asked the waiter whether this was, perhaps, an "Al Capone" day parade that was causing the awful racket. Glancing casually over the parapet he matter-of-factly replied,

"Oh no, those are just some of the guests leaving Hugh Hefner's party."

We understand that Mr. Hefner's neighbors in this

beautiful and conservative part of old Chicago feel that
Mrs. O'Leary's cow was a bit previous. We were telling
a group of friends about this party when we came home
to California and one of the men asked Jimmy,

"You took your wife to that party?"

"Sure," replied my nice husband, who is a pussycat
. . . not a bunny.

"Wow," exclaimed this same man, "taking your wife to
a 'Playboy' party is like going fishing with the game
warden."

One usually associates parties with gaining weight, but
the best party we ever went to came as a direct result of
losing some. Three or four times a year I go to a beauty
spa in Escondido, California called "The Golden Door" for
a week of diet, exercise, and beautiful regression. Going
to this wonderful place is like being a kid again in the
world's most luxurious camp. I originally took off for the
"Door" after Jimmy facetiously remarked that I looked
like I belonged on the critical list at Slenderalla. Really,
there is no place like this anywhere. It is deep in some of
the most beautiful country in the state. It was built for the
sole purpose of relaxing, refreshing, and reinvigorating
from sixteen to twenty females at one time. The rooms are
charming. Each one is perfectly appointed and has been
done in a different period. The food is exquisite. It is hard
to believe you are dieting. There are one-and-a-half maids
per client. The people who run the place are dedicated.
There is an aura of love that completely permeates "The
Golden Door," and best of all, it's such fun!

All the thinking is done for you. Your program of events
comes in on your breakfast tray. Exercise, body massage,
steam cabinet, vapor room, facial, scalp massage, water
exercise every day and modern ballet, Yoga, beauty and
health lectures, water ballet, ballroom dancing, etc. two
or three times during the week, and at the end of your

stay, pedicure, manicure, coiffeur and make-up, and off you go to your loving spouse looking like a doll!

It was such a hit that the husbands got a little jealous so they instituted Mens Week. Perhaps you saw the pictures of Jimmy, Aldous Huxley, and Bob Cummings luxuriating there in "Life" Magazine. They run it for the men exactly as they do for the women. Nothing is changed—even the things they give us to wear, from the terry cloth togas, the gold leotards, down to the pink sweat suits and the little sandals—all are worn by the guys. After the second day I called Jimmy to find out how he liked it.

"Gee," he told me, "I like it. Maybe I shouldn't. Those calisthenics with those golden wands! That honey massage, the bleach on my elbows, the vapor baths and that rigorous hour of interpretive dancing through the woods. I feel like I'm going through basic training to be a fag!"

He loved it! He's been going back for Mens Week every time they have one which seems to have settled down to every three months. He loves everything about it. When he came home that first time eleven pounds lighter and looking like he did when we first met, I couldn't have been more thrilled. I couldn't wait to dance with him! I'd been waiting for sixteen years! It was about time! I asked him,

"How did you like your ballroom lessons?"

"Oh, I was the best," he said, "I loved it! I got the gold star!"

"Well," I exclaimed, "just let me put on a cha cha record and we can try it out right now."

"Oh, I can't dance with you," he said, "I can only dance with my partner, Mr. Albert Sloane, a big industrialist from Chicago!"

Once while in Chicago, in the privacy of our hotel suite, my husband and Mr. Sloane who towers above him put on an exhibition of Latin capers witnessed only by Mrs.

Sloane, myself, and an amazed waiter from room service. Jim once had the nerve to say to me,

"If it weren't for the stupid mores of this country, Mr. Sloane and I could win every trophy—why we could go on the Arthur Murray Dance Party and get the grand prize—except he looks so good in a sheath, he shouldn't lead!"

A funny thing about the clients who unflab themselves at "The Golden Door" is that some of them come there in cliques. One week there was a group from San Francisco. Another time a gang from La Jolla. Then once a really large mob from Texas. Mrs. Clint Murchison of Dallas, Mrs. Otho Sparks of San Antonio, and Mrs. Jake Hamon, also of Dallas, were among them. Jim called that group the low calorie Fort Knox.

Nancy Hamon and I became fast friends and have managed to go to Escondido together a number of times. The last time we were there, Nancy told me about the annual costume ball she and her oil millionnaire husband have been giving for many years now. They take over one of the country clubs in or around Dallas and as many as eight hundred and fifty people, who come from all over the world to attend, have been their guests. The parties have been interesting and unusual. A lot of thought as well as money has gone into them. One party was a Toulouse Lautrec theme, for example. Another was an East Indian affair. A third, which they gave in the garden of their own home, was a Louis Quatorze garden party completely in period. But this year it seems they were running low on ideas.

"I know what you can do, Nancy!" I told her. "It wouldn't work in our town because it's too close to home. But it might be fun for Dallas. Why not do a silent movie party! You could come as Theda Bara, and maybe Jake can be Erich von Stroheim! I've always been a student of 'silents' and I have loads of antique movie magazines and I could send you to lots of places to do your research!"

Nancy was delighted! And so, after staying up long after "Lights Out," we started to really plan it all.

I sent Nancy to the Curator of the Modern Museum in New York whom I knew would be of tremendous help. I told her to see Palmer Finchley, my old friend, who has charge of theatrical and motion picture scrapbooks at the great public library on Fifth Avenue and 42nd Street. We went through many of my ancient books and periodicals and came up with sketches of how the rooms in the country club should be arranged and decorated. And then Nancy, who is a born producer and who was meeting Jake in New York the day after our week's stay was up, went off to do her research and organize the party which every year is their big cooperative family project.

I arrived in Dallas, a few days before the Hamon costume ball so that I, too, could help with the decorating. To me, that's the best part of any party and that's why I love to give them. From the time I left home in California until I returned to it, I don't think I had more than ten gulps of real air. I went from the air conditioned Neiman-Marcus to the air conditioned country club, to the air conditioned Neiman-Marcus, to the air conditioned private houses, to the air conditioned Neiman-Marcus, and then in and out of the air conditioned automobiles that everyone in Texas drives to the air conditioned Neiman-Marcus.

When it comes to hotels, my husband's tastes are very traditional. When we arrive in a strange city, he heads like a homing pigeon for the oldest and most conservative hotel in town, and once the hotel is taken over by a chain, as far as he's concerned, it's like the daughter who has sinned—it ceases to exist! For years he waged a one-man war against Conrad Hilton, crying to all who would listen that he'd desecrated Beverly Hills with that huge juke box he'd erected called "The Beverly Hilton." He's refused to enter its electronic portals to this day. I can hear him now on his usual tirade—

"When I go into a hotel I don't want the door opened by some damned electric eye! I want a doorman! A real doorman! Like the one we met in England who said, "I'm a doorman and I'm proud of it! My father was a doorman! My grandfather was a doorman! You want to know something?—I'm part door!"

"And when I check into a hotel I want to talk to a desk clerk . . . not an I. B. M. machine."

Once he was forced to stay in a brand-new hotel. As usual he signed for everything. When the actual bill arrived, he was so enraged by the undecipherable notations and the holes punched by their tabulating machine, that he sat down with my tiny manicure scissors and very carefully manufactured a few holes of his own that were calculated to give the I. B. M. machine a nervous breakdown. He sent it back to them stating that the bill was incorrect and added, "I think one of your robots has his claws in the till!"

So you see, most of my married life I have spent in hotels like the "Ritz" in Boston, the "Belleview Stratford" in Philadelphia, the "Fairmont" in San Francisco and the "Pochertrain" in New Orleans. I have spent so much time in hotels like these that I think of myself as a sort of an elderly "Eloise"—and may I add, Jimmy is one heck of a nanny!

Nancy and Jake had me booked into the newest showplace hotel in Dallas. Dallas rather reminded me of the Beverly Hills of twenty years ago, with its low white buildings in the bright glaring sunshine. When my air-conditioned taxi approached my air-conditioned destination, I saw a tall skinny building looming up before me. It had a real doorman! And he gave my luggage to a real bellboy! And I registered at the desk with a real clerk! The bellboy took my luggage. He deposited me in an elevator, pushed a button and was gone. I was alone in this thing which was rising at a terrific rate of speed! It went up . . . and up . . . and up! Finally at long last it stopped at the top floor. Nancy and Jake did me a big favor. They got me a view! When it stopped I leaped out, almost into the arms of the smiling bellboy who was waiting for me. He escorted me to a really beautiful room, parked my luggage, said thank you for the tip and disappeared. He was the last human being I saw!

I looked around. Over by the windows was a long cart upon which rested a magnum of champagne in a silver cooler with two champagne glasses (Jim was expected later by plane), a bottle of Jack Daniels, a bottle of Scotch, a bottle of Vodka, a bottle of Gin, a huge basket of fruit, a giant box of candy and a beautiful flower arrangement. There were cards hanging all over,

WELCOME!!!
NANCY AND JAKE

It was a lovely welcome!

It was such a warm afternoon I went over to open the windows and get a breath of fresh air. Not a chance! Sealed shut! I went into the bathroom and opened one of the two "medicine cabinets." Ice cubes tumbled out and arranged themselves into a silver ice bucket, which upon the touch, leapt into position. I saw a little bronze sign which read, "For television in bed—press below." I pressed below. A door in the wall beside the bed opened and a T.V. set came skittering out across the floor and came to rest at the foot of the bed. The controls, naturally, were embedded in the night table. I picked up the phone to get the operator. Not a sound came through the instru-

ment. I jiggled it! Nothing happened! Just dead silence!
I had a moment of panic! All I wanted was to find out
where the stairway was hidden so I could avoid ever riding in that speeding box on a string again. Was I stranded?
Then I saw a panel of buttons. They read:

```
LONG DISTANCE  .....  PRESS HERE AND DIAL
LOCAL CALLS  ........  PRESS HERE AND DIAL
ROOM SERVICE  ......  PRESS HERE
VALET  ...............  PRESS HERE
FLORIST  .............  PRESS HERE
BEAUTY SALON  .......  PRESS HERE
BARBER SHOP  ........  PRESS HERE
HOUSEKEEPER  .......  PRESS HERE
```

When Jimmy checked in and took a look at the telephone
dial, he said, "When a traveling salesman checks in,
there's probably a button that lights up and says,

```
BROADS  ..............  PRESS HERE."
```

After we looked over our Southern space capsule, he
said it reminded him of the story of the Martian who
landed here on earth, walked into a beer joint, took a look
at the neon cigarette machine and said, "What's a nice
girl like you doing working in a joint like this?"

I've never met a girl who didn't dream of someday
going to Neiman-Marcus, which in Dallas is known merely
as "The Store!" I went, too, that first day . . . for one
yard of yellow ribbon for my 1916 ingenue pompadour
. . . which was all I needed to complete my costume for
the ball. Going to Neiman-Marcus for a yard of yellow
ribbon is a little like asking Picasso to paint your porch!

"The Store" was sixty-five cents away from the hotel. I
felt like a devout Moslem must feel as he is about to view
Mecca for the first time. I don't know what I expected—
but it wasn't what I got. The cab came to a stop in front
of a corner deep in a dreary section of the Dallas business

district, and there in front of me was a very ordinary
corner store, rather old-fashioned looking and about the
size of the leading department store in any midwestern
city. I don't know what I expected—the Taj Mahal with
escalators? I was no sooner in the main door when two
charming lady clerks approached me. One of them said,
"Welcome to Neiman-Marcus! Youah new here, am ah
raht?" I admitted I was and asked how they knew.

"Oh," she replied, "we can always tell. We get to know
awall oweh customers. Now what can we do foah you
owah—oh ah you just lookin' arawnd?"

I blurted it out!

"I need a yard of yellow ribbon," I admitted!

"Well," she said, "now that's too bayad. We gave up
ouah yahd goods and notion depahtment quaht a whahl
back. You'll have to go to the fahve and tayen."

I had no idea where that might be. "Honey," she told
her fellow clerk who up till now was merely helping her
smile, "go ask Mrs. Simmons if we can escort this charmin'
strangeh to the fahve and dahm."

In a moment we were on our way. They walked me to
the dime store, waited, smiling all the time while I bought
the ribbon. They stayed by my side through the entire
transaction and even escorted me out of the store. I was
very grateful.

"Thank you very much, ladies. That was very nice of
you. Well . . . er . . . ah . . . it's getting late . . . almost 5:30. I'd better be getting back to the hotel now."

"Oh no youah not, honey! Youah comin' back to the
stoah with us!"

And so to my amazement I was "grinned" all the way
back to Neiman's where they plopped me into a big fat
chair.

"Now you just sit thayah whahle we call you a cayab!
You see you would have been stranded. It's closing tahm

down heah. Cabs must be called in Dallas—they'ah not allowed to pick up in the streets!"

How sweet of them! The least I could do was open a charge account.

"Can ah get you a floweh pot, honey?" they asked as they plumped the pillows behind me.

What on earth would I do with a flower pot? But it was so nice of them to ask. Not wishing to offend their southern hospitality, I said I'd love one. The flower pot was delicious! It was lovely Wedgewood, and contained a baked Alaska with a little fresh Garnet rose stuck through the meringue. It's a specialty of their Zodiac Room, and I wish I had one now! Then, as I sat in my comfortable chair, eating my flower pot and waiting for my cab, the two darling salesladies gave me a Neiman-Marcus shopping bag with handles to carry my dime store ribbon in. As I sat there contentedly with the mellifluous southern voices drawling in the background, I could have sworn I heard banjos playing in the distance. I couldn't help thinking—what a shame that nice General Lee lost the war . . .

The clerk's voice was asking me, "Now, foah the charge account—how do we make it out, mayam? Youah name, please?"

I started, "Mrs. Rhett But . . . I mean Mrs. Jim Backus."

The night of the masquerade ball arrived and with it Jimmy and his secret costume in a giant box under his arm. He went into his room to dress. It didn't take me long to get into costume. I wore a short yellow voile nightgown and peignoir, which somehow looked like an old-fashioned young girl's dress. Under it I had a stiff ruffled petticoat and a pair of dead white leotards. (They wore chalk white stockings in those days.) I had a yellow ruffled garter below one knee, and my white kid ballet slippers had little yellow bows on them. I wore a long red "fall" to match my hair which was done in a high pompadour in front and where the true met the false in the back, I had attached a large yellow bow from the Dallas dime store. With my stylized 1916 movie make-up, my little gold locket and my no-polish nails, I felt I looked the part.

Not long after I finished dressing, the connecting door opened and there stood the largest, fattest, silliest "Buster Brown" I ever saw—complete with Dutch bob wig and hoop. So off to the ball we went! We followed the search-lights in the sky out to the Northwood Country Club and up their wide and beautiful drive. There at the entrance was a shined-up ancient Rolls Royce which Jake Hamon had had towed to the club in honor of the occasion. In the front seat, in full livery, sat the Hamon butler with a silver bucket and a bottle of champagne. Standing in the back, straight as a Ramrod was our host, in a Prussian general's uniform, a monocle in his eye, an Erich von Stroheim look on his face and a glass of champagne held high, to greet his guests. For two hours he welcomed people from this vintage car. Driving up in marvelously imaginative cos-tumes were the guests—some of them in antique autos, gigs and surreys. A few of the "cowboys" were on horse-back and a large stagecoach drawn by six white horses, pulled up containing a dozen Keystone Cops, who tum-bled out of it followed by their bathing beauty escorts led by Mrs. Clint Murchison. I was impressed . . . but Jim said the least she could have done was to borrow a locomotive from her Allegheny railroad.

The entrance hall was designed to look like a set from a Theda Bara movie. There were tiger skins, vases full of peacock feathers, fringed shawls draped on tables, beaded lampshades and mother of pearl tabourets. Lying full length on her stomach on a pile of Oriental rugs was that celebrated vamp, our hostess, being fanned by a giant bejeweled Nubian slave who looked suspiciously like a fellow who had been liberated from the locker room for the evening.

Over all of this played a flicker machine, giving the entire club the effect of a silent movie. The first room was designed to look like a nickelodeon, with signs like "Ladies Will Please Remove Their Hats," etc. and with coming attraction posters all over the walls. Nancy had had old stills blown up and she and her artist son-in-law had painted the borders and done all of the lettering. Over the bar was a movie screen which, when we entered, was showing "Tillie's Punctured Romance." This room opened onto the ballroom where they were dancing to the music of Louis Armstrong and his band. We got across the room by fox trotting to the strains of the "Shiek of Araby." There were more posters of those blown up stills on these walls, too. In fact they were everywhere. In the room next to the ballroom there was another screen over the bar on which were projected endless slides of old motion picture stills. Then came the room with the buffet, which made the barbecue scene in that celebrated extravaganza "Giant" look like a television film! At each table were directors' chairs with the names of the "great ones" hand lettered on the back, by the Hamons, of course—"Robert Flaherty," "Rex Ingram," "Mack Sennett," "Cecil B. DeMille," "D. W. Griffith," "Frank Borzage," and the like.

The service was perfect! They had thought of everything! They even had one attendant whose duty it was to take messages on all the car telephones, and instead of place cards there were megaphones. There were about eight hundred defenders of the Alamo present, and I must say they came on strong! There were endless Rudolph Valentinos in every one of his roles, there were William S. Harts and Jack Hoxies, and Mary Pickfords and Baby Peggys, and Greta Garbos and Ham Hamiltons, and Bobby Vernons and Charlie Chaplins galore. There was one man with four heads who came as the Warner Brothers—Albert, Sam, Harry, and Jack. There was a Roy D'Arcy complete with handkerchief. There was one small person done up as "Farina," an inspired female who came in deep mourning with a sheaf of roses in her arms as Ditra Flamé—the lady who mourns at the grave of Valentino each year on the anniversary of his death. But our favorite costume of all was a gentleman who actually looked a lot like William S. Hart. What he had done was very simple. He was an oil driller, and he simply came in his working clothes. All that he had added was a pair of false eyelashes. To say that that was understated was an understatement!

At dawn as we were leaving, we overheard a terrible argument. A slightly smashed guest in a "Buster Brown" suit just like Jimmy's was screaming at the cloak room attendant, "Wheh's mah hoop?" The attendant asked him if he was sure he had had a hoop.

"Had a hoop," he roared. "Sure! Ah rolled the damned thing all the way from mah ranch to this club and in through that dooah. And ah checked it raht heayah!"

"Well, I'm sorry, sir," apologized the attendant. "It's not here. But don't worry, sir—we'll send you one in the morning."

"In the mohnin'?" screamed the blasted "Buster Brown," "that's no help! How the hell am ah goin' to get home tonight?"

6 excess baggage

ONE NIGHT last February, Henny and I were spending a quiet evening at home when suddenly she said,

"Has it occurred to you, darling, we still have never been to Europe?"

I must say I was taken aback, so I replied brilliantly, "By George . . . you're right," thinking that would be the end of it.

But not at all. Henny, in her best birddog style, countered with, "Why don't we go? Don't you think it's about time?"

With that I sat her down and patiently told her: "First of all, darling, we can't afford it. To put aside a lump sum of money just for traveling, and no business reasons whatever, is ridiculous—let's face it! We're both extravagant, we admit it. And besides, all our money is tied up in cash. I can understand that you want to travel and visit glamorous places. So I'll tell you what. This summer it looks like I'm gonna be making a submarine picture in Little America, and you can go along. Only remember . . . on a submarine you can't sleep with the windows open. HA, HA!"

I looked up at Henny for my laugh, only to be met by one of her death rays, capable of stopping a Sherman tank at two hundred yards. I then decided to use pure logic.

"Darling, listen, we're above a trip to Europe. Let's face it! That's for squares. You want culture? You're up to your derrière in culture. We don't have one friend who doesn't have at least one Picasso or Renoir or a Nell Brinkley. And honey, we spend all our time with writers, artists, and musicians. Our whole life is one 'bal masque.' And as for the Riviera . . . we live on the Riviera. Swim? You've got a heated pool! You like to gamble? You drive every day on the freeway. Even our marriage is European. I am the master and you are subservient to me. Your job is just to be feminine and beautiful, while I make all the major decisions—and my word is law! So, pass me some 'crêpes suzettes' and my 'café au lait,' and don't you think it's a little cold to be eating in front of the house on the sidewalk?"

The next morning, as I was looking at the plans of the Queen Elizabeth and picking out our adjoining cabins with the aid of a travel agent, the phone rang. It was Charlie Goldring, our business manager and Tim Cratchit, calling from his high stool.

"Jim," he screamed. "I don't know how to tell you, but there's been a run on your checking account during the night. Someone converted $10,000 of your hard-earned cash into travelers checks. I have a call in to Elliott Ness."

"Never mind, Charlie, I'll be down later and explain!" It was much too late! It was Bon Voyage baskets for all.

From that day on, the phone started to ring, chums dropped in, friends stopped us on the street, and strangers wrote letters offering advice. And all the advice was different!

One said—

You're sailing March 16th? Are you out of your mind! At that time of year England is a swamp!

Another said—

March 16th? Oh darling, that's divine! You think you have seen green—wait till you see England in the spring!! It's heaven —and Paris? April in Paris. There's no other time. My wife, Bruce and I go every year!

Then—

Of course, you're going to fly! There's no other way. Right over the Polar cap! Take two Nembutols—and some of that free champagne—and the next thing you know you're there. And the best part of this is you'll never know you left Los Angeles!

Still another—

Of course, you're going by boat! You're not going to do anything asinine like that flying bit. The best part is getting there. But for God's sake—not on one of those dreary "Queens." The "Liberté"—it's a running ball! And that food and the toy balloons! Of course, you know it's the old "Bremen." Its falling apart, but who cares.

Once again—advice

There's only one way. Go over by boat! But for heaven's sake—not on the American line!! If you go American, you might as well stay home! Then fly back, because by then you've had it!

More—

I hope you have sense enough to fly over and then take the boat back. Get there and have your fun! But man, will you need that five days at sea to unwind!

Another tipped us—

Just take one suitcase and buy what you need over there.

An effete one simpered—

You better take everything, sweetie! You never know what the weather will be like at that time of the year. And who wants to waste time with fittings. If you don't fly, the luggage is free on your ticket anyway. Just take all your oldest clothes and jewelry. Buy all new clothes and jewelry when you get to Europe. Everybody knows things are cheaper over there, darling! Then send all your American things home in an old suitcase. Mark it "Laundry," and wear your new European stuff throughout the trip. Then you can go right through customs without paying any duty!

Our lawyer called—

Don't dare to try to sneak anything through customs. Just declare everything! Even declare things you haven't got and they'll give you a break, because they'll be so impressed with your honesty.

An expatriot claimed—

Don't let them book you into any of those fancy hotels. Stay at a "Pension!" It's the only way you'll really get to know the people. And besides, it's so much cheaper!

A movie star gushed—

My dear, stay at the best hotels—the ones you've always heard of. That "Pension" stuff is for the birds! No room service! They can't understand a word you say! And who needs that "chamber pot" bit!!

A libertine advised—

Don't drink water—just drink wine! Remember that picture of the little boy. It's true! Ne jamais pas de l'eau!

A disciple of Gaylord Hauser claimed—

Drink the water! It's perfectly all right. So you get a little dysentery. It'll keep your weight down.

Henny's mother insisted—

They have no paper over there! Take lots of Kleenex!! It has
to double, you know!!!

Well, all advice to the contrary, one salient fact stood
out. Henny does not fly. People have cajoled her. Airlines
have offered her free trips. Factual-minded folks have pre-
sented her with statistics proving that you are safer in a
plane than in your bed—but still Henny will not fly. Her
fear of planes makes absolutely no sense, because believe
it or not, she adores blimps! She once got into one to have
her picture taken for publicity, and before she knew it she
was airborne. She refers to them as "soft trains." But try
booking a blimp to Europe!

Two weeks before she was to leave for New York,
Henny started to pack. Since we were taking only trains
and boats, the weight of the luggage was of no considera-
tion. The fact that she could take as many pieces as she
wanted was like giving whisky to an Indian. Most of
her luggage was inherited, particularly one giant-sized
steamer trunk with a fading label which read "S.S. Mer-
rimac," and a slightly smaller trunk which bore the tag,
"S.S. Monitor." (Henny's family had played it cool during
the Civil War.) She had those—plus a Jules Vernean carpetbag which when entirely empty weighed over sixty
pounds. There were also numerous portmanteaus, valises,
and hampers. It looked like the luggage of P. T. Barnum
and Jenny Lind. All this plus a jewel case that only Willie
Sutton could open.

To give you an idea of what she took with her, the vast
regions of the carpetbag alone were stuffed to bursting
with a full manicure set, a professional collapsible hair
dryer, twelve giant cans of hair spray, a gallon of con-
centrated shampoo, a sack of hair curlers, a dozen cakes
of soap, and seventeen boxes of Kleenex. It looked like a

CARE package for Max Factor. She had a hat box, which in addition to her hats, contained a wig, a false "bun," a "fall," some bangs and a Spanish shawl comb and mantilla for her possible audience with the Pope.

She packed one full wardrobe in that giant trunk to be shipped ahead—and another full wardrobe for the same occasions in the smaller trunk which was to go on the trains and ships with her. I asked her why, and she replied,

"That's my 'cover' wardrobe."

So, naturally I asked,

"What's a 'cover' wardrobe?"

"You know what a 'cover' wardrobe is! That's so I'm covered in case they lose my big trunk in the shipping, see!"

Which once again proves the old adage, "you ask a foolish question, et cetera." She was also carrying with her a basket full of magazines, books and back issues of newspapers that she had not had time to read, crossword puzzles that she had not had time to work, a mink coat, a sable stole, a vicuna coat, a normal umbrella, and a folding umbrella. Oh—and of course, her typewriter, her portable bathroom scale, and her fading wicker hamper which bore the legend, "Happy Sailing, Scott and Zelda."

I feel the success of any good marriage depends on the partners outslying each other. Henny, as a woman, has her share of little tricks, but occasionally I come up with a dandy. This time I really outfoxed her!

The day before we were to take the train for New York, I booked myself on the Danny Thomas show, which would mean I would have to do the show, fly to New York, and just make it the morning of the sailing. Let Henny worry about transporting her two tons of assorted goodies via the "Iron Horse."

Let's face it! She's crossed the continent so many times

that when she boards the Super Chief, it's like a class reunion. Everyone from the engineer to the conductor, the dining car steward, the bar man, the waiter and the porter are known to her by name. She is the patron saint of the Santa Fe—a latter day "Harvey girl," the toast of the Vista-dome! In fact she is the only girl who has ever posed for the cover of a timetable.

Well, she made it to New York, but not before having a disastrous upset while changing trains in Chicago. As she was dashing from the Dearborn Street Station to the La-Salle Station (or is it the other way around?) her luggage exploded in the true "Phineas Fogg" tradition, just as she was boarding the "Twentieth Century." They had to hold up the train while the baggage master and eight porters, who were handsomely tipped, gathered enough rope, cord, string, chains and Scotch tape to encircle all her impedimenta.

At times like this my wife drives me crazy! She called me the minute she got on the train and from their radio telephone told me the whole story.

"Darling," I said, "you've just got to get rid of that potato famine hand freight. Tell you what! We've gone this far—we've spent this much money—so when you get to New York get yourself brand new luggage. It will be cheaper in the long run!"

"New luggage," she retorted, "why you hedonistic hot-head! I'll just get the bell captain to get me some good strong leather straps with locks in them."

"Henny!" I screamed, "why don't you just throw all that junk of yours away and get new stuff! It's much simpler."

"It's not much simpler," she told me. "I'm used to this luggage. I know where everything goes. Besides, you're always accusing me of being extravagant, and I'm getting good and sick of it!!"

She hung up in a huff. It just never occurred to her that the cost of this lengthy short-wave telephone call from that fast-moving train, where every time she cleared her throat the rates went up, would have more than paid for a pretty darn good set of matched luggage.

I arrived a week after Henny on the day of the sailing at 7:00 A.M. We were to sail on the Queen Elizabeth at 11:30 A.M. I rushed to the hotel only to be greeted with,

"Mrs. Backus checked out—she left last night!!"

"She left last night? Where did she go—and where's all that luggage?"

"She took it with her," they told me, "and furthermore she asked if you would be kind enough to tip the five bellboys and the driver of the van." I panicked.

"Did the boat sail last night? I thought it went out this morning!"

"It does, Mr. Backus, but Mrs. Backus boarded last night! And," he added with a knowing wink, "Mrs. Backus got the Cunard people to stretch a point."

I rushed down to Pier Ninety. It took two hours to push my way through the jostling, surging, pushing mass of humanity that accompanies any sailing. From no sleep on the plane and the startling news at the hotel, plus my bewilderment by the turn of events, by the time I got on board I felt pretty much like the pigeon that got caught in a badminton game.

Wearily I fought my way to Cabins A-75, A-76. I opened the door to the drawing room. Soft music was in the air. Books and magazines were arranged on the tables. Champagne was cooling in silver ice buckets. There were vases full of beautiful flowers everywhere. A wheelcart full of hors d'oeuvres was standing by. My dream girl emerged from the bedroom, immaculate in her satin hostess gown and said,

"Come in, darling, and make yourself comfortable. I've been waiting for you!"

I slumped into a chair and accepted a sliver of pickled eel and a cup of steaming tea.

I knew better than to ask how she had gotten on board the night before. The telephone rang and Henny answered it.

"Hello," she purred. "Yes—yes, he's here. He just got here. Oh yes, we're quite comfortable, thank you. What's that? By all means! No—no, it's perfectly all right now, Captain. Anchors Away!!!"

7 fun and games

WE ADORED every bit of our European trip. It was worth waiting for. This trip was designed in heaven. Nothing went wrong.

The best part of it was going over on the Queen Elizabeth. We loved traveling by ship so much that next time we're going to take a cruise so we can "live in." Those five wonderful days on the "Liz"—which is what she is called by those in the know—made us both blithering Anglophiles. We had a ball the whole way!

The only thing we feared was the British press. We had been warned that they were tough on American performers, particularly the Hollywood variety. I had been advised to expect quite a few interviews, since "Mr. Magoo" had been a long-time favorite and "I Married Joan" was currently Number One in popularity on British television.

First of all, let us straighten out one base canard—that English cooking is lousy. I admit we expected to get nothing else to eat except "Toad-in-the-Hole," "Bubble and Squeak," and "Roly Poly Pud," but I must say we could not have been more wrong.

Henny and I have eaten in some pretty fine restaurants both in America, and, as of now, in parts of Europe, but we have never had such food as the wonderful fare served in the Verandah Grill on the Queen Elizabeth. The Verandah Grill is a small private restaurant located on the top deck at the very stern of the boat (we hope our marine phraseology is right, because we heard one bewildered lady say to a sailor, "Pardon me, but is the ocean upstairs?"). The Verandah Grill seats about one hundred people, by invitation only, and charges a dollar-and-a-half cover charge per person per meal. We were delighted to be asked—and it was worth it.

The guests of the Verandah grill on our particular trip looked like they had been cast by Somerset Maugham. Among them were the incredible Lady Nora Docker, her husband, Sir Bernard, and their entourage, Prime Minister MacMillan's daughter and her husband, an out-of-work king, a Dutch planter who explained to us the ordeal of managing a four-hundred-thousand-acre plantation and having personally to perform executions and brain surgery at the drop of a machete, and a wealthy cannibal chieftain who asked for the passenger list instead of the menu.

There was no formal menu in the Verandah. The boast was that they could make anything. They had no problem with Henny, who ate nothing but fresh Iranian caviar. She ate jars and jars of caviar, sometimes varying this with a side order of "blini." It was the first time in her life that she could have all the caviar she wanted—and for nothing too! She was like a little girl in a candy store. One night for want of something better to do we figured out how much caviar she had consumed in five days. It turned out that the Cunard people had taken a $182.00 loss on her passage. If nothing else, this trip accomplished one thing. It made her so sick of caviar that, now, even seeing it on a menu causes her to blanch. She is so fed up with it, she is campaigning for planned parenthood for sturgeons.

I was more of a challenge. I ordered everything from bird's nest soup to Shashlik. It became a contest between our waiter and me. At every meal, I ordered something that I was sure they would be unable to prepare. But I couldn't stump the experts. One night I really laid it on them. I said,

"First of all, bring my wife a moonshine cocktail."

Then I calmly ordered.

"Black-eyed peas, corn pone with black strap molasses, hominy grits and chittlings and possum stew." I sat back to gloat.

As our waiter turned on his heel I gasped,

"Are you really going to bring that?"

"Certainly, sir," he replied. "It's our integration special!"

"Fun and Games" started the moment you opened your eyes. Pushed under your door you would find the *Ocean Times,* in early Gothic print. This contained all the current news written in typically British fashion. We especially liked the weather report, to wit:

BRITISH WEATHER
Cloudy with intermittent drizzle
Further outlook: Similar

There was also a daily quiz that no one could ever answer in full. The prize for the one answering the greatest number of questions correctly was (as it was for any event on the "Liz") some Queen Elizabeth cocktail glasses.

The first day's quiz was a "True or False."

R.M.S.   "QUEEN ELIZABETH"
TRUE OR FALSE

1. The earth revolves anti-clockwise   . . . . . .
2. Capetown is the capital of South Africa   . . . . . .
3. William Booth founded the Church Army   . . . . . .
4. Joan of Arc was burnt at Rouen   . . . . . .
5. Berlin stands on the River Oder   . . . . . .
6. Napoleon is buried at St. Helena   . . . . . .
7. A Springbok is an insect   . . . . . .
8. Andrew Carnegie was a philanthropist   . . . . . .
9. Puccini was born in 1858   . . . . . .
10. The Queen Mother lives at Marlborouth House, London   . . . . . .
11. Mr. Fahrenheit invented the thermometer   . . . . . .
12. New York was founded by Stuyvesant in 1653   . . . . . .
13. Alfred Nobel invented high explosives   . . . . . .
14. Longfellow has a bust of himself in Westminster Abby   . . . . . .
15. Stockholm is known as the "Venice of the North"   . . . . . .
16. The penny farthing bicycle was made in the 1850s   . . . . . .
17. Koala bear is only found in Australia   . . . . . .
18. Young pike are called pickeral   . . . . . .
19. Purcell wrote the British National Anthem   . . . . . .
20. Honolulu is on the Island of Hawaii   . . . . . .

A prize will be awarded for the first correct or nearest correct solution received at the Purser's Bureau. The competition will be closed at 5:00 p.m. today, and the winning entry, together with the key solution, will be posted on the Notice Board outside the Purser's Bureau at 6:00 p.m.

Passenger's name_____
Room No._____Time handed in_____

We hope the reader does better with this than we did. There was also a shipboard shopping guide which was heavier than our phone book at home and a daily "Programme."

R.M.S. "Queen Elizabeth" Friday, March 18
PROGRAMME OF EVENTS

A.M.

7:00—Gymnasium and Squash Racket Court open
    Swimming Pool available from 7:00 a.m. to 1:30 p.m.
    and 4:30 to 7:00 p.m. (weather permitting).
10:30—Recorded Concert   Ballroom
    Violin Concerto in E Minor (Mendelssohn). (Yehudi
    Menuhin). Romances: No. 1 in G Maj; No. 2 in F Maj;
    (Beethoven) (Yehudi Menuhin)
    (Concerto) The Berlin Philharmonic
      Orchestra
    (Romances) The Philharmonic   Conductor:
      Orchestra   Wilhelm Furtwangler
10:30 to 11:00—HOSTESS RENDEZVOUS
    Miss Elizabeth Sayers will be in the Starboard Garden
    Lounge to discuss any shipboard queries you may have.
11:30-11:55—Totalisator on Ship's Run   Prom. Deck Square
11:30—Ray Baines at the Hammond
    Organ   Main Lounge
11:55—Tote closes   Prom. Deck Square
    Winners paid shortly after noon or at the Purser's Bureau

P.M.

3:00—Table Tennis Tournament   Prom. Deck
    commences
3:15—Melody Time   Main Lounge
    Ray Baines at the Organ
3:45—Music for Tea Time   Main Lounge
    Marcel Torrent and the
    Palm Court Orchestra
4:30—Organ Classics   Main Lounge
    Ray Baines at the Organ
6:00—Cocktail Hour   Observation Bar
6:00—"The Voice of America"   Main Lounge
    News Broadcast
6:15—B.B.C. News Broadcast   Main Lounge
8:30—Orchestral Selections   Restaurant

Marcel Torrent and his
Orchestra

8:45—"The Voice of America"   Main Lounge
News Broadcast

9:00—B.B.C. News Broadcast   Main Lounge

9:15—Ray Baines at the Organ   Main Lounge

9:45—Horse Racing, and Bingo

10:30—DANCING   Ballroom
and the "Queen Elizabeth"
Glee Club

Marcel Torrent and the "Queen Elizabeth" Dance Orchestra

A.M.

12:30—STARLIGHT ROOF CLUB   Verandah Grill
introducing our Charm and personality girl:
GRACE RICH
Tommy Wade and the "Queen Elizabeth" sextet

CLOCKS
Clocks will be advanced 20 minutes at
5:00 p.m., 11:00 p.m. and 2:00 a.m.

TODAY'S MOVIE PROGRAMME:
at 4:30 and 9:30 p.m.
"WHITE WILDERNESS"
by Walt Disney
"Cow Dog"

Do you realize that these activities could go on for a
full twenty-four hours, as the rule of the Verandah Grill—
once it turned into the "Starlight Roof Club"—was that
you could eat, drink, and dance as long as you liked. Some
of the more hearty souls danced, drank champagne, and
ate kippers until 7:00 A.M. . . . or until the "Squash
Courts" opened. With all these planned activities, the
"Queen Elizabeth" was, as far as we were concerned, a
high-church Catskill resort—sort of a floating Grossingers.
From our observations on this giant Cunard liner, we
came to the conclusion that the British people are hooked

on two things—organ music and bingo. Wherever you went on board, the air was permeated with the musical artistry of Ray Baines playing roundelays on his giant Hammond organ, with all the stops out. You could hear him in the swimming pool—even in the steam room. Henny says she once heard him under the dryer!

Equally as loud as Ray Baines and his organ was the bingo game which started promptly at 9:45. The giant salon was jammed. You couldn't get a seat. It was packed with enthusiastic Britishers eagerly waiting to play "plain old bingo," "traveling bingo," "once-across-the-top," and "housy housy" (whatever *they* are). Permanently in charge of the bingo game was the young assistant purser. He had an odd ritual. After the cards were sold and all were once again seated, he held up a large felt bag which was the cue for a thousand voices to shout in unison, "and now . . . we . . . SHAKETHEBAG!!!" Now the calling would begin, but instead of simply calling the numbers, the assistant purser would embellish each one with, "It's Legs Eleven . . . Betty Grable!" "It's Times Square . . . Forty-two!" "It's Downing Street . . . Number Ten!" "It's a jar of pickles . . . Fifty-seven!" "The Number Life Begins at . . . Forty!" "It's Jack Benny . . . Thirty-nine!" "It's the United States . . . all Forty-eight!" We asked him about that.

"What about Alaska and Hawaii?" we said.

"I'm terribly sorry, sir," he replied, "it's traditional—that's the way we learned it in purser school."

The second night out I was approached by the smoking room steward who asked me if I would be good enough to auction off the ship's pool. I said I'd be glad to, but I didn't quite understand how it worked. He then explained it to me.

The ship's run is from twelve noon to twelve noon. At midnight, the captain sends down from the bridge his estimate of the day's mileage. He gives the steward a range of twenty numbers within which he thinks the ship's mileage will fall. For example, he will give a range of between 615 and 635 nautical miles that he thinks the ship will make that day. At twelve noon the following day, whatever mileage the ship has traveled is the winning number of the pool. These twenty numbers are auctioned off the night before. If the bidder feels that the captain is not going to make it within his estimated range, he can buy "low pool," or if he thinks the captain is going to exceed his twenty mile range, he may buy "high pool."

The pool auction was always held in the small smoking lounge after "Bingo" attracting the more seasoned and, needless to say, well-heeled travelers, who bought their tickets to the pool with whatever was handy—cash, checks, travelers' checks, I.O.U's et al. This, because the ship's pool was an unscheduled event, was kept in an empty cigar box to be handed intact to the lucky winner.

Many legends have sprung up around these ship's pools, which often involve tremendous sums of money. There's the tale, perhaps apocryphal, about the gambler who bet everything he had on "low pool" (in other words, that the ship was not going to make the captain's low estimate). So, to insure himself of winning and to slow the ship down, he threw himself overboard!

After I consented to be the auctioneer, the steward said:
"Sir, I hope yours is a 'proper whopper!' "

The steward and his staff are very enthusiastic about the pool because, first of all, a certain percentage of it goes to the seamens' fund. And then, it is good for business, since the winner usually buys drinks for the eighty or ninety losers. And, of course, it is also considered cricket for the winner to tip the staff quite handsomely.

I must say the pool I auctioned *REALLY* turned out to be a "proper whopper," because Lady Docker and her

caravan were out to outbid Lord John Tredegar and his
coterie who were trying to prevent a syndicate of rich
Americans from buying up everything in sight. It was an
unheard of 50 pounds for openers, followed by the wildest
kind of bidding. This was not as foolish as it seemed, because these were all seasoned travelers who had access to
the logs of other crossings, and knew what the ship had
done for the past twenty years on the same day under
comparable weather conditions. So, believe it or not, the
highest number, 739, which was auctioned last, was the
number none of the three camps wanted. The "Queen
Elizabeth" had never come within five miles of that, and,
to make this number an even worse buy, we were running
into a heavy sea. When I called "739" I was greeted with
a stony silence. The three camps had had it. Suddenly I
heard a voice say, "I bid 15 pounds!" It was Henny in her
best "Nick the Greek" tone. This must have started a chain
reaction, for another feminine voice said, "I'll up it to 16!"
This set off spirited bidding between eight or nine frus-
trated females who had been just sitting there all night. It
also amused the three heavy-betting rival camps, who sat
back as if to say, "Let the ribbon clerks have their day!"

Well . . . Henny bought it for the incredibly low price
of 38 pounds. Do I have to tell you??? During the night,
the captain explained later, the ship turned south due to
icebergs, caught a following swell, was goosed by a
friendly typhoon, ran into some slippery kelp, and later-
aled off the Sargasso Sea causing it to hit 739 right on the
nose. So Henny now had one more addition to her luggage—a cigar box full of travelers' checks, personal drafts,
bundles of pound sterling, and the mortgage to an ancestral English castle called "Old Herman on the Hole."
Henny was now so drunk with power she tried to buy
The Queen Elizabeth—but the Cunard people wouldn't
break up a set!

I envy my wife her ability to quickly adapt to places and people. It is a much slower process with me. By the time I had gotten used to life at sea, we were landing in England. By the time I got used to England, we were on our way to France. By the time I got used to France, we were in Italy. And so it went! It wasn't until I got home that I started getting used to Europe. My enjoyment was almost entirely retroactive.

Henny, on the other hand, had a complete rapport with the crew. After three days at sea, they had their own private jokes. Some of them they had carefully rehearsed. Like she and Munn, the head steward, would carefully thread their way into a group. Then she would say:

"Steward, what time's the mutiny?"

"Don't worry, madam," he'd reply, "the men are revolting."

"Revolting," she'd say . . . "they're disgusting!"

She had another routine worked up with one of the eager apple-cheeked young assistant pursers. Since there were always a number of people doing business around the purser's desk, she would approach and quietly ask:

"Young man . . . could you direct me to the mizzenmast?"

He would counter with:

"I'm terribly sorry, Madam, but the mizzenmast is mizzen!"

Pretty awful!

To the staff captain, Mr. Goodier, whom she ran into in the lounge, she said: "I just saw the captain in the bar —and now you're here. Who's minding the store?"

"No one," he stated, "this old girl knows her way by herself."

When she ran into the captain a little later, she said: "When are you going to let me steer?"

"Tomorrow," he topped her with, "when we get to Southampton."

"Southampton," she cried . . . "do you mean it's taken us five days to get to the end of Long Island!" The captain and crew adored all her bad gags.

We were due to land on Monday the 21st of March. So Saturday night was the ship's gala, which included what many passengers had been preparing for—a fancy headdress contest. These headdresses were to represent the titles of popular songs. The purser, to get the shy ones and lazy ones into the spirit of things, would, as was their custom, lend them already made-up stock hats—like a tray with a ribbon that tied under the chin, bearing upon it a teapot and two cups, as, naturally "Tea For Two,"—that sort of thing. The captain, the head purser, Lady Docker and Henny and I were to be the judges. That afternoon we were sitting on deck with two friends we had met on board, Inga and Reggie Sugden from Sheffield. The Sugdens manufacture 30% of all the scissors, knives, and surgical instruments used in the world. Reggie typified the charming conservative English businessman—far removed from his "lampshade-on-the-head," American counterpart.

I don't know why, but we all suddenly decided that Reggie should enter the headdress contest. I guess we got stubborn about it, because Reggie in a hat contest seemed so charmingly out of character. After three drinks and quite a bit of persuading, he agreed.

"But," said Reggie, "I'm not going to wear one of those frightful ready-made-up things I've seen on every damn crossing."

Henny jumped straight up in the air, shouting, "I've got it . . . my red wig!!! It was made for you, Reggie!!!"

This was the year of the wig, and many ladies had them. They were considered very chic, and they were certainly practical. When there was no time to have her hair done, Henny would slap on her really quite beautiful auburn wig.

She whisked Reggie down to her cabin and pinned him

into the wig, and for further effect, added her long be-jeweled Egyptian earrings. That night was long to be re-membered. There were many imaginative and amusing headdresses. But when Reggie Sugden glided across the floor bathed in a baby blue "spot" to the tune of—what else —"A Pretty Girl Is Like A Melody," it was all over!! By acclamation!!!

(I remember screaming at Henny when she paid $500.00 for that wig. But if ever a wig paid off . . . it was this one. Reggie not only presented her with his prize, the "Queen Elizabeth" cocktail glasses, but two months later an alligator case with her name in gold arrived from Shef-field, and in it was a complete set of magnificent Royal Crown Derby steak knives and forks.)

As we staggered off to bed again at the crack of dawn, Henny said,

"Now, remember darling, tomorrow is the day before we land, and I've got to get all our packing done. So right after dinner I'm going to do just that, and then I'll climb into bed, because I want to feel great tomorrow. Remem-ber we land in England on my birthday. And, sweetheart . . . this will be one birthday I'll long remember." And it was!

As for getting to bed early, there wasn't a chance. Our British friends, in their best "Fun and Games" tradition, arranged an informal surprise birthday party for Henny in the grill. The only thing is, instead of waiting for mid-night, they jumped the gun and started surprising her at 5:00 in the afternoon. It still looked like a fairly early evening when one of our gang won the Ambrose Light pool of several hundred pounds. With cries of "Strong Drink For My Men!!! We Ride At Dawn!!!"—the party carried on.

The last thing we saw as we tooled off to bed at 5:00 A.M. was a bearded Israeli actor and a Saudi-Arabian shiek, complete with burnoose and scimitar, arms around each other, sharing a slab of Polish ham, a magnum of vintage Mogen David Wine, and singing "Auld Lang Syne" with a Levantine beat.

We finished all our packing about an hour before we were to dock.

"Thank heavens that's over with," said Henny. "Now we can simmer down for a few minutes."

She jumped up! "My God, my wig! Reggie forgot to give it back. Please run up and get it from him, sweetie! He can keep the earrings if he likes them, but get that wig. If it rains I'll need it!" I did as I was told.

"Just look at it," she said. "I can't pack it away like this or I'll never be able to wear it. I've just got to dress it, Jimmy . . . and you know what . . . I forgot to bring the wooden block. You have to put it on."

I started to yell, "Now, wait a minute, Henny . . . . . !"

"Now, now, now, darling . . . sit still and look out the porthole at the green pretty countryside and I'll just use your head for a block. Now, please darling, I have to put it up on curlers"—AND SHE DID, TOO!!!

About this time there was an unfamiliar lurch and a grinding sound. I said, "Henny, get me out of this damn wig! I think we've landed!"

"Just sit quietly, sweetie, I'm not finished yet. I've arranged with the steward to tell us when it's time to go ashore."

Well, the next thing I remember, there was a sound like an explosion. Our door literally burst open and thirty-two gentlemen, some with cameras, stormed into the cabin . . . and there I sat in that crazy red wig! We had forgotten all about the British press!

8 tea and strumpets

LONDON SEEMED smaller than we expected. Big Ben wasn't very big. The streets weren't very wide. Buckingham Palace wasn't very formidable. Why Buckingham Palace wasn't even in a park of its own! It stood close to the curb and seemed not so much a palace, as simply the biggest house on the block.

But there was a delicacy about this city and, though it seemed smaller than we expected, it was a joy to behold. We both felt so at home there; it was almost as though we had been to London before.

It was all so beautiful!! This was the first day of spring and the day was doing its best to prove it. When we got to our rooms high in the Dorchester Hotel, we looked out and saw an astonishingly lovely sight. Every window as far as the eye could see had a window box full of bright yellow daffodils. Each rooftop and canopy top had been transformed into a gaily-colored, geometrically-designed garden, planted with yellow daffodils, China-blue hya-

111

cinths and red, red tulips. The effect was breathtaking. How was this achieved? Is it a law? Do they have window box and rooftop clubs? Or have all these people simply got the taste and energy to want to make their city bloom with this magnificence. And if that's the case, why can't New York do it too? Every time we go *there* it seems uglier than the time before. Is there a deliberate plan afoot to louse up that once magnificent city? Why did they ruin beautiful Park Avenue? Who caused the erection of those hideous office buildings nobody wants to rent? How about that building with the soap bubbles constantly foaming up off the roof. And that Seagram building that looks like it's made out of gold lamé bricks. This structure, unlike the product that built it, is not going to improve with age. We hear that if Mr. Zeckendorf ever comes up with the money, he has some real goodies planned. One is to be a mother-of-pearl motel complete with heliport on top, plus a formica landing strip. When Kruschev was so furious about not being allowed to visit Disneyland, someone should have simmered him down by pointing out that his legation at Sixty-third and Park looks out on Disneyland in spades. After visiting New York with its gaudy new buildings, it's a relief to get back to quaint conservative Hollywood with its vine-covered mortuaries and ante-bellum pizzerias. Granted we have the Brown Derby restaurant which is shaped like a hat . . . but it has tradition. It has stood, unmolested in all its fedora loveliness, for over thirty-five years. Why, they haven't even had it blocked!

The first night we were in London we decided to really do the town. We dressed! We had tickets to a hit show. After the play we were going to the "Caprice" for supper with Margaret Leighton and some other members of the cast and then on to "Les Ambassadeurs" for champagne and dancing. As we emerged from the lift in our hotel, we saw him! Our first real Englishman of quality!! Even from his back you could tell he was to the manor born. We speculated on what his title might be. He was impeccably attired in tails, top hat and an Inverness cape.

I said, "Look, Henny, when it comes to that certain something, the English have got it and we haven't. And we're not about to get it either. Notice the way his clothes hang on him. I could go to the best tailor in the world and never even approach that casual elegance. Look, darling, look at the way he is requesting a cab from the doorman with his stick. Oh, and look . . . look at the way he is tossing the doorman a coin. I'll bet he's on his way to Buckingham Palace, and furthermore . . ."

Before I could finish my sentence, Henny had left my side and was deep in an embrace with this gentleman. It's all right to be an Anglophile, but I felt she was carrying it a bit too far. She swung him around, and I saw his face for the first time. It was the face of our friendly Beverly Hills credit druggist, Leon Schwab. As he put one daintily slippered foot into the cab he shouted,

"Anything I can do for you, old bean, during your sojourn in the kingdom?"

"Yes, you rat fink," I yelled back, "send up some Dr. Scholls foot pads!"

May I say it wouldn't be too hard to become an Anglophile. For openers, take their cabs. First of all they're painted a decent respectable color—black! And the way they're designed makes sense! They're so comfortable and tall. You can almost stand up in them. The designers of our billious yellow beetles should be taken by the scruff of the neck and forced to ride in one of their own monstrosities, clad in a lady's dress, high heeled slippers, carrying a handbag and a few parcels and wearing a large hat, then firmly escorted to London, dressed in that same outfit and put into a London taxi. That way maybe they'll get the message. It might be a little hard for General Motors and Chrysler to explain a bevy of automobile executives clad in ladies' dresses, high heeled slippers, carrying handbags and parcels and wearing hats . . . but on the whole it would be well worth it.

In London, with only the barest help from the doorman, a lady can step gracefully into a taxi without ruining her hair or her gown. In an American cab the doorman has a really difficult struggle fitting the lady into her seat. It takes such bodily contact, there is often the danger of impregnation. Thank heavens for those heavy overcoats our doormen wear. If it weren't for those, we'd be breeding a race of children born with ear muffs and a whistle. A lady in an American taxi is in the same position as a Rhesus monkey in a space capsule.

Another thing the London cabs have and we certainly do not is smooth level floors. We have deep wells on either side of the drive shaft, so if it's raining or snowing, the cab has six or seven inches of slushy water for you to slosh around in. Then, when you emerge from the cab, your feet look like open-toed Daiquiris. In an American cab the leather of the seats may be split, the windows broken, the doors hanging by one hinge—but there, leering at you, beautifully framed and lighted like a painting in the Louvre is a photograph of your driver. Why, when he goes to have this beautifully exhibited picture taken to be seen by the thousands of people who enter his cab, must he show up unshaven and glowering and wearing on his head a tweed cow flop? And furthermore, inasmuch as his unpronounceable name is up in lights, why doesn't he change it? Actors do!

Next, let's take the American versus the English bathroom. Nowadays in America they've gone to great lengths to disguise the fact that a bathroom is a bathroom. A bathroom used to be white—a gleaming surgical white. It had dignity and a suggestion of clinical urgency, and you knew at a glance where everything was and what it was for. Now, it is all done in the muted tones of a cocktail bar. A bathtub used to stand there majestically on its four little feet. Now they are casting it in a one piece mold so it looks like a porcelain bagel. The shower, of course, has disappeared completely. That's in a room of its own somewhere, and the donniker has been so streamlined it looks like the bucket seat of a Ferrari.

The English have retained the bathroom in all its classic snow-white purity. The towels are huge, white, fluffy and numerous. And what's more they're warm! They're hung on big bronze heated towel racks. What a great idea! This is a far cry from those American hotels where you're afraid to use more than one towel at a time, because you have the feeling that Conrad Hilton is looking over your shoulder—counting! And that wonderful heavenly scented English soap, the size of a football! Quite a difference from those little slivers carefully wrapped in paper with those printed commercials, advising you to come downstairs and dine in the Aaron Burr room.

I must admit that in our English bath there also seemed to be all sorts of strange, severe looking brushes, belts and straps that we never understood. It gave us the feeling that we had perhaps stumbled into the trophy room of the Marquis de Sade. However, beside the tub in our hotel was a large mahogany and leather chair. It had arms and was shaped to fit every contour of the human body. Over this was draped a huge terry cloth sheet. I couldn't figure out its exact function till Henny told me that was what your valet wrapped you in when you emerged from your bath. A man could do worse than to sit and relax in a towel-covered chair after a tub. And what's more, they still have that chain! That wonderful chain that I remember from my grandmother's house. It gives one a sense of power. You are in charge of the situation. The situation is not in charge of you. It's like driving a car with a stick gear shift.

And, while we're on the subject, whatever happened to privacy in the bathroom? Nowadays in an American bathroom, according to television advertising, that seems to be the most crowded room in the house. The whole family gathers there. They admiringly cluster around dear old dad while he shaves. Mother simpers something about, "Would you believe it, I've got a cold!" Grandma with the blue-gray hair shows up with a sincere intern who assures her that she can break the laxative habit if she follows an algebraic equation that only a nuclear physicist can understand. Then to further invade the privacy of the once private American bathroom, an Ivy League announcer appears with a man with a transparent head full of hammers and knotted ropes. This same man has a pari-mutuel window in his stomach where you can bet whether Bufferin or Aspirin will come out ahead. To add to this terrible tableaux, which by now has reached the proportions of Ben Hur, a dreadful child comes bursting in with some thundering news! "Look ma, no cavities—but I'm pregnant!!!" Now tell me, who needs functional togetherness!

It's an amazing thing to us that for a nation of skinny people, the English eat constantly. They have breakfast, elevenses, lunch, tea, dinner and supper, with assorted cups of tea and watercress sandwiches in between. All this is interspersed with numerous Scotch and sodas, tankards of ale and pink gins. It seemed rather odd to us since the average American will stick pretty close to his drink of either Scotch or Bourbon with an occasional Martini, and on special occasions, perhaps Champagne or Brandy, that the English, who as a nation are rather addicted to Scotch, will switch around helter skelter and drink anything that's offered to them—rather like a high school girl at her first prom. Back in the days when I used to belt the booze, I would only drink Scotch and soda and it had to be a certain brand. If, however, I was caught in the morning with a severe case of the "whips and jangles," the only thing I could get down was a beautifully made Brandy milk punch. I noticed many times in English clubs, groups of men ordering pre-luncheon drinks. One would order a Sherry Flip, another a Split of Champagne, the third a Pimms Cup complete with cucumber, the fourth, perhaps a Scotch and Splash, and the fifth a glass of Claret. Then they would exchange sips like clubwomen having luncheon in Schrafts.

How do the English people, particularly the men, stay so slim? Their intake on an average day has got to be over ten thousand calories. Not only do they seem to be eating all the time, but their meals are so much larger. Dinner, for example, in a fine restaurant, is table d'hôte, which is almost unheard of in a comparable eating house in America. Much to our surprise, we found many, many fine restaurants in London. Our favorite was the "Caprice," which is now considered to be one of the finest in all of Europe. A normal table d'hôte dinner in this lovely place would be, to give you one example, as follows:

A dazzling assortment of hors d'oeuvres

Dover Sole

A separate course of giant asparagus from Brittany (which is eaten with the aid of huge tongs)

Tenderloin of beef with sea salsify and baby peas

Belgium endive salad

Wild strawberries and Devonshire cream

Petit fours

Miniature French pastries on a large tray at the table

Mints and coffee

And then a savory—perhaps sardines or caviar on toast. Well now!!

If you're wondering how they can afford it, this dinner I have just described, cost roughly $3.60 per person. One night when we were back in our hotel doing the "Dodsworth" bit, Henny in negligee and me in my evening pumps, cross garters, and dressing gown, reviewing the evening, I sat at the desk and figured out on paper what we had spent for the night's entertainment. We started out at the Dorchester where we bought a few drinks for some friends. This was not exhibition drinking, mind you, but each one had his share. Henny and I then went to a hit show (in London the curtain goes up very early, so you dine after the play). After the theatre we had dinner at the Savoy. Then we went to Helene Cordet's private club for a brandy or two. Then on to Les Ambassadeurs again for dancing and a bit of Champagne. The whole thing came to $38.00 including cabs, where I think I was guilty of overtipping, not to mention the fact that Henny spent several pennies. Instead of saying, "Excuse me while I go to the powder room," in England, the ladies say, "Pardon me, while I spend a penny." Because that's what it costs to go!

One of the things I was constantly amazed by was the fact that I was recognized wherever I went in London. It seems that my old series "I Married Joan" had been playing on British television to great success—even greater, I believe, than in America. One of the reasons for its popularity was its time slot. There are only two channels in England, and "I Married Joan" went on at eight P.M. with only one show as opposition—a knitting lesson. I once asked an executive of the B.B.C. what kind of a rating we had and he looked at me blankly and said, "Rating?" So, I said, "Yes, in America there are various systems of ratings to find out how many viewers a show has. Like 'percentages of sets in use,' a 'breakdown of share of audience,' and an 'automatic trendex.' I must say I never understood it and I don't think the fellows who make up the polls do either, but the sponsors gauge a show's success by these various systems."

The executive I was talking to looked at me in amazement and said, "Well, I can't give you any figures like that, old boy, but I'm sure everyone, if they were at home and their valves were in good shape, watched you. I can't imagine what else they would do. As for your competition, the knitting lesson, the only ones who watched that were the Queen Mother and a few fags, so I imagine your rating must have been ninety-nine point nine eight."

Not bad when you consider that the Nielson highest rating of the Nixon-Kennedy debate was sixty-seven.

Although we were in England "on holiday," we did do a few television shows. First, because we were asked, second, because I'm a ham, and third because I wanted to confuse the man from Internal Revenue. (Right here I would like to say that we told the income tax people the major purpose of our European trip was to gather material for this book. So, to those of you who have read this far, may we say "thank you" for not making liars out of us.)

Essentially the variety shows and the dramatic plays for T.V. are staged just about the same way that they are in America. But, oh how different are the interview shows? We were on one called "Late Extra," which is broadcast over the "Associated Rediffusion Network." Why it is called that, nobody knows, including its founder, Mr. Associated Rediffusion. This show was England's answer to the Jack Paar show—and like the Jack Paar show, you only get a token payment. But that token payment was handed to us right after the show . . . in Cash! What a thrill!!! Remember the old days when everybody got paid in cash? Remember that nice brown envelope full of crisp green bills? Whatever became of money? Imagine doing a show and getting paid off immediately in real cash! I never felt that way, even on the Jack Paar show with that $320. It went by check a week later to Charlie Goldring, our business manager. I never even saw any part of it. I remember saying to Henny when we got our brown envelopes full of money in London, "You know something, when I get back home and start filming my new series for N.B.C., I think I'll make them pay me every Saturday afternoon in cash. Can't you see the telegram I'll get from General Sarnoff—'What are you . . . some kind of nut or something?' "

Vivian Kellems . . . move over!!!

The modern system of taxes, particularly in Hollywood, has certainly screwed up our sense of values. All that we were taught as kids like, "A penny saved is a penny earned," the legend about "the grasshopper and the ant," and that bit about "storing nuts for the winter," are of no earthly use whatever today. If you practice them, you've got to wind up in Alcatraz or, even worse, at a table on the left-hand side of El Morocco. For example, if you earn a certain amount of money by October the first, you don't dare make one cent after that date for fear of being put into another income bracket. This is a far cry from what we were taught as children. For example, my fee for getting up and saying a few words at a banquet, unless it is for charity, is roughly $2,500. But come November, if someone wants me to drool a few pearls after the demitasse all he has to do is take me aside and assure me that someone will slip me a hundred dollar bill out of petty cash, and I'll leap at the chance like an out-of-work fire-eater snapping at a Crêpe Suzette. I remember a couple of years ago I had an offer in December to do a filmed television show which was okayed by Charlie Goldring because the money was deferred to the following year. That same evening Keenan Wynn and his wife dropped by to drink a dollop of bourbon and eat a pound of walnuts. It's not that Mr. Wynn is hungry. It's just that he gets great satisfaction from cracking them with his bare hands. That night Keenan told me he had an offer to do two T.V. shows in December which would net him roughly $10,000.

I said, "Look, Keenan, I'm no Joseph Galbraith, but if you made $138,000, this being December, you need another $10,000 like you need a hole in your head. Why don't you do like me and see if they won't defer it until next year. I'm sure they will because it's the same company."

Cracking three walnuts at once in his bleeding hand, he replied, "Gee, that's a wonderful idea. I'll do it! No . . . I can't! I can't do it! If I don't get that $10,000, I won't be able to buy a Christmas tree!" Any questions?

Back to Associated Rediffusion and "Late Extra." Unlike American television shows, they arranged to have us picked up in a limousine. We got to the theatre at 10:30, about a half hour before we were to go on the air. In America they leave you to your own devices to nervously pace a drafty corridor which smells like a handball court. Here, the chauffeur escorted us into a delightful tap room right off the studio where the performers always gather to be served hors d'oeuvres and drinks by a butler and a bartender.

About two minutes before air time, the master of ceremonies, who looked like he had just come from a regimental review of the cold stream guards, said to me, "I say, old boy, why don't you have the bar man mix you a triple. Take it right on stage with you. Hide it in your wife's mink muff. I've got mine tucked behind the microphone."

Can you imagine this in America where they live in dread of someone showing up slightly swacked on a panel show? Why, they practically greet you at the stage door with a Sen Sen Geiger counter, and once on the air they make innuendos (with all the charm and grace of small boys behind a billboard smirking over a copy of *Captain Billy's Whiz Bang*) about the fact that someone might have had a Martini!

Now, I must leap to the defense of American television. If you are on an interview or talk-type show and you are telling a story, and the commercial or station break is coming up, the emcee usually protects you by saying,

"Jim, I'm sorry I don't want you to go any further, because I've got a commercial coming up. Just wait till it's all over and you can pick up where we left off, or if you want to, you can start all over." But not on British T.V. I remember telling a joke and in all due modesty, I had the audience in the palm of my hand. I was coming right up to the punch line of the story when the cheerful emcee said,

"Well, Jim, shall we terminate the interview?" The screen went to black. They cut to a closeup of Big Ben and the entire network rediffused.

Compared to London't night life, Paris is as exciting and orgiastic as a De Molay picnic. For example, Henny and I hit a little night spot called the "Eve Club." We went through the usual ridiculous ritual of becoming members. In London every spot is a private club, but anyone, it seems, can become a member—that is if he has the initiation fee and the imagination to make up two fictitious names as references. I remember our two references were Dr. Albert Schweitzer, 622 Lumumba Avenue, Casavubu Heights, and Mrs. Mamie Eisenhower, housewife, Gettysburg, Pa.

The "Eve" was quite a club. The whole room looked like a giant pin ball machine, as hidden lights kept flashing on and off. The striped satin walls were sprayed with gold and silver glitter. The ceiling was a fake sky with silver stars, each containing a tiny flashing spotlight, plus a lovely fat grinning celluloid man in the moon. As I remember it, the central theme of the decor was a mural of Adam standing in front of Eve, covering himself with a flounder. Compared to the "Eve Club," New York's Copacabana looks like the Sistine Chapel. The whole thing had a sort of prohibition era flavor. The tables were about the size of postage stamps with tiny dim lamps and little wooden noise makers, and, so help me, confetti to throw at the show girls.

I turned to Henny and said, "What'll you have to drink?"

The head waiter, who showed up in a skin-tight tuxedo with a wing-tipped collar and a butterfly tie, said, "I'm sorry but we serve no liquor after midnight on Saturday night. So might I suggest a pot of tea . . . or perhaps a lemon squash . . . or would you care to look at our menu. We have a lovely table d'hôte dinner."

I turned to him and said, "No, thank you. Zelda and I have had our dinner. Just bring us two Ginger Ale setups."

Suddenly the floor, which was made of translucent blocks of glass, lit up from below in a blaze of light. This illuminated the entire club and we suddenly realized that Henny was the only female on the premises. The whole room was jammed with table after table of men. Just groups of English businessmen, eating table d'hôte dinners, drinking tea and wearing suits made of roofing material. And why not? The room temperature was a comfortable thirty-six. I'm sure that during the day the room doubles as a place to hang meat.

At last the show was on. Eight completely naked ladies wearing comfortable shoes and fruit compotes on their heads danced on. The cold gave them goose bumps, and the bad lighting made their veins stand out. They looked like animated road maps. In the first number, the group which was billed as the "Nudie But Nicettes," did a mirror dance, wherein they flashed little hand mirrors on faces of the men at ringside and they whined in a nasal twang (since naturally they all had colds) about how lonely they were and how they wished they had someone to dance with, at which point forty of these staid British businessmen jumped on to the floor without any coaxing at all, as if they had been rehearsing for months, and tossed the young ladies from one to another, giving some of the nudies a severe case of mat burn from their suits. When the number was over, the men returned to their Roast Joints, while the girls, no doubt, dashed to the infirmary, suffering from shock and exposure.

Now the master of ceremonies appeared—believe it or not—a lady! She was dressed in a Ruby Keeler hand-me-down, complete with black sateen jockey shorts, tails, top hat and tap shoes. Her material was early Milton Berle.

"Of course, you know since they have taken the girls off the streets, they all have flats. Well, two of the girls were discussing this novel method of practicing their profession, and one said to the other,

"'Ow didje dew larst week, Alice?"

"Oh, just foine, dearie, oi took in a hundred and twenty-five quid."

"Gross?" she asked.

"No, I think his name is Lipschitz."

The sound of the hammers was deafening. Two of the ringside tycoons carried her bodily to their table where they toasted her in mint sauce.

The astonishing thing about the "Eve" is that these places are flourishing all over London. They go on at night as well as all day long, with emphasis on the "Strip Tease." Business men meet there for lunch and possibly even for elevenses. I guess the English really like their TEA WITH STRUMPETS.

9 hey madam—your sign fell down

In Paris Henny and I did all the usual things. We tramped through the Louvre, climbed to the top of the Eiffel Tower (Henny hates elevators), Friday-nighted it at Maxims, bought a painting in Montmarte, had a fitting at Dior's, sampled the onion soup at Les Halles at dawn, and had lunch with Art Buchwald.

We got to Paris the hard way. Since Henny doesn't fly, we went all over Europe without ever leaving the ground, which is some kind of record nowadays. We left London on the night train. At Dover the train was strapped into the bowels of a channel boat where we swayed and jerked and slithered nauseatingly around all night long. It was like being on a demented Staten Island ferry. We never heard such noise—such agonizing screeches and groans and muffled screams. We still think the boat was propelled by galley slaves whom they brought out of hiding as soon as they thought we were safely asleep. The train ride was, incidently, a wonderful way to lose weight, as they kept

it at a crisp 110 degrees and the only bed linen was a
combination sheet and blanket which I am sure was made
out of General Pershing's overcoat. After surviving this
trail by rail and stepping for the first time upon French
soil, instead of uttering the classic, "Lafayette, we are
here!" we cabled our broker to buy us one hundred shares
of T.W.A.

I felt a little strange in Paris. There was that language
barrier, and in Paris, as in New York, you have the feeling
that no one gives a damn whether you live or die.

I couldn't wait to get into our sumptous suite in the
George Cinq where I immediately took to my bed. I fell
into a deep state of malaise from which there was no rous-
ing me. I had no appetite and I was afraid to venture
forth. Henny tried her best to rouse me from this tangled
state of mind that had seized me. She brought me little
delicacies. She got me 3-D French postcards for my stereo
viewer. She even tried do-it-yourself shock therapy—she
stuck my big toe in a light socket (sometimes home reme-
dies are the best). Finally she solved it. Her cure was very
simple. She just hired some urchins who were working
their way through the Sorbonne to stand under my window and chant:

"Vive Monsieur Magoo!"

I thanked her soundly . . . for once again I was a tiger!
I left my couch, ready for action.

"Here, here," my practical wife said, "you can't go out
there! You can't speak one word of French. What if we
get separated? Then, what would you do?" And she was
right! She sat me down with my book of *Phrases Most
Commonly Used and Needed,* which had been given to
me by that citizen of the world, Peter Ustinov. I learned
from it in phonetic French such handy phrases as,

"Please put the carriage of my aunt into the lift."
and

"*Regardez! Do not wash the golf balls in the bidet!*"
and

"*Mon oncle has la grippe. Please apply leeches,*"
and the very necessary

"*The bustle of la bonne femme has fallen into the bouillabaise.*"

Henny, who loves to cook, has always wanted to take a course at the celebrated Le Cordon Bleu. I talked her out of it. I said, "Honey, why bother? You're doing so well in the cooking school in Beverly Hills. Why, you led your class in advanced defrosting! Besides you can't drop everything and go to some cooking college in Paris! And you're married! You're too old to go through all that pledging, sororities, the homecoming cookout for Betty Crocker and all that! The next thing you know you'll be pinned by some young chef, and I won't even . . ."

"You idiot," my wife said to me, "it's not that kind of a school! Besides there isn't time for it this trip anyway. So don't worry about it. But I do want to sample some of the haute cuisine. So let's go to some of the great eating places, huh? I think I can learn a lot that way and then maybe after dinner I can go backstage to the kitchen and meet the chef. How about that?"

This discussion was causing me to salivate like one of Doctor Pavlov's dogs—and being loaded with American Express green stamps, I said, "Honey . . . you name it! Anyplace you want. Where to tonight?"

"That shrine of great food!" she replied, "the Saint Peters of gastronomic delights! The Taj Mahal of Epicures! The place where I've always dreamed of dining, darling . . . Le Tour D'Argent!"

I said, "Angel, if you'll stop those Cole Porter lyrics, I'll take you."

I realized while I was getting dressed that night that I was in Paris and it was April. April in Paris! All the Paris clichés were rapidly coming true. The chestnuts were really in blossom. The twilight was actually mauve. The air was soft and sweetly scented, and full of romance, and believe it or not from the street below came the sound of a children's carousel. It was almost too much. Henny wafted into the room looking like a dream. I took her into my arms.

"Angel, we made it. We're in Paris! It's Spring and we're in love! Tonight, this will be our city!"

As we started out the door Henny said, "Jimmy, just one thing before we leave this room. Take off that straw hat, tuck in your lower lip, stop singing 'Every Little Breeze Seems to Whisper Louise'—and for heavens sake, wear your Paris garters on the inside."

When we got out of the little lace lift and stepped into the lobby I said, "Honey, you go into the bar and wait for me, and I'll telephone Le Tour D'Argent and reserve a table."

"You can't do that, darling," she said. "This is Paris! You can't just phone and reserve a table all by yourself. What do you think the concierge is for?"

"The what?" I demanded.

"The concierge," she told me. "I read all about it, so I know exactly what you should do. Now look, you go to the desk and introduce yourself to the concierge. Then cross his palm with silver before you even tell him what you want. That way he'll give you service. Oh, yes . . . and the bustle of la bonne femme won't be necessary. The concierge always speaks English." She floated into the bar, leaving me for the first time, completely alone.

In chain of command the concierge is roughly the equivalent of the professional first sergeant in the Army. If you've ever had any dealings with things military, you find out that if you want anything done, and done immediately and well, you go to the sergeant or to the general. If you try anyone in between, you're wasting your time. The concierge is the most important person you will deal with, no matter what your accommodations might be in continental Europe. First-class hotels to pensions—wherever you stay—the concierge is in charge of all activities, from the purchase of a postage stamp to reservations on trains, planes, ships, in restaurants, night clubs and theatres, to the hiring of cars and guides, and for the lone traveler . . . a dainty knock on the door at three a.m. These fancy head porters have the same snobbishness and pseudo-haughtiness that you only find in a head waiter. If you sense that your concierge doesn't like you or approve of you, just move out! Move out, because you haven't got a chance! No amount of tipping, threatening, cajoling, long talks with the manager or phone calls from the Embassy are going to help you. Just move! However, the best way to establish a line of communication with him is to be firm. Walk up to him with the equivalent of five American dollars in your hand and say,

"I am Mr. So-and-So, and I am going to be with you for x number of days, and I'm going to need your help!"

It won't be difficult! Intimate that if he serves you well, there will be another tip at the end of your stay. You may have lost your self respect, but you have gained a concierge. In all the travel books and guides that we have ever read, they make one horrendous error. They tell you how much to tip, but they never tell you when. Everyone assumes that one tips at the end of the stay. Not so! It doesn't seem to work out that way. Look at it this way. The concierge, the maid, the porter and the valet have never seen you before and there is a fighting chance that they'll never see you again. How do they know what you're going to give them at the end of your visit—if anything. We had our own system, and it always worked. For example, the moment we checked in we rang for the maid, gave her the equivalent of an American dollar, and intimated that there would be more to come. From that moment on the baths were drawn, the beds turned down, buttons were sewn on, shoes were shined. Why, they even gave us toilet paper instead of the usual Butterick patterns. We found one cardinal rule. When in doubt, tip first!

After giving the concierge a propitiatory offering and being assured of a fine table at Le Tour D'Argent, I joined Henny in the bar. The George Cinq bar was the only place in Europe that for some strange reason was exactly as both Henny and I had imagined it to be . . . small, quiet, and elegant and always filled to capacity with beautifully dressed members of the international set. We were fascinated by the people at the next table. There was a military man seated there who, from his kepi, I judged to be at least a field marshall. On his left was a fierce Bedouin sheik busily sucking on a hookah and nibbling some skewered lamb. Next to him sat an ascetic red-robed papal knight and beside him was one of France's leading couturiers magnificently turned out in fuchsia morning clothes, who was languidly stroking a Siamese cat which looked terribly chic in its jeweled dog collar and earrings. In addition to these four, and dominating the table, was a gentleman, obviously the host, whose back was to us. He was in animated conversation—a man of obvious fire and magic. When he at one point turned almost to profile, we could make out his Pince Nez ribbon of red, white, and blue. I was never so impressed.

"Look at that man, darling," I told my bride. "I'll bet he's one of those Greek shipping magnates, or maybe even a merchant of death!! Could he be an international spy? Is he selling munitions to either side? Or, he might be a former President of France. Look, look, sweetie, doesn't he look to you like Leon Blum?"

"What are you . . . some kind of a nut or something," she answered. "It's not Leon Blum . . . It's Leon Schwab, our friendly credit druggist from Beverly Hills—better known as the Basil Zaharias of the Nembutal set."

"Gee, he's everywhere," I exclaimed. "Maybe he's establishing a cartel for bedpans."

Actually wherever we went in Europe Leon Schwab was there or had been there or was just about to arrive. For many years Henny and I have been ardent and devoted customers of Les Frères Schwab apothecary, and possessors of one of the biggest tabs carried on their books. In the fifteen years we have lived in Hollywood, I don't think we have ever been completely even with these "talcum powder tycoons."

It was in one of the Schwab drugstores that Lana Turner was discovered. Sydney Skolsky, the columnist, uses Schwab's drugstore as his office. Caesar Romero gets his kicks mixing sodas at their fountain. These pharmacists have been catering to the movie colony for over thirty years. In our town, Schwab's is not merely a series of drug stores. It's a way of life!

One day Henny was shopping for a beaded evening bag at a rather obscure atelier in downtown Paris. The bag she fell in love with was priced at well over two hundred dollars. At the time she was carrying considerably less—and they don't welcome credit cards. I won't bore you with the fact that a man Henny thought was one of the beaders, turned out to be Leon Schwab. But there he was! He admired the bag that Henny wanted.

"Why don't you take it?" he asked her.

"I don't have enough money," said my wife.

"Tell you what I'll do," she continued. "I'll take it and you can put it on my tab."

Henny is the only dame in the world who bought a

beaded bag in Paris and charged it to a Beverly Hills drug store.

Well, the night was young and our car was waiting. So off to dinner! Le Tour D'Argent was high up in a building overlooking the Notre Dame cathedral and the Seine. The George Cinq concierge had done his job well. We were ushered to a table jutting out over the beautiful river. The setting was magnificent! There were two giant menus lying on the table, but, before we even had a chance to read and decide, the maître d', with all the deftness of a Hialeah tout, had talked us into their specialty—pressed duck. We never had a chance. He snowed us with the fact that the duck had been hanging there with our name on it and, as a momento of this auspicious event, they would give us a piece of stamped paper bearing the number of the duck we were about to eat. Each duck eaten in this restaurant since the day it opened has been carefully catalogued and numbered. I turned to the maître d' and asked,

"Each duck is carefully numbered? What do you cook them in—an I.B.M. machine!"

Henny gave me a wifely drop kick to the shins. In less time than it takes to cook an egg, two revolting platters appeared, bearing half-raw ducks swimming in ice-cold blood. It's all right to press a duck, but this was ridiculous. These poor fowl had been pressed to the thinness of a wafer. I'm an actor and I've spent a good part of my life on the road and I've eaten some pretty lousy food. May I say that the food at Le Tour D'Argent is right at the top of my list. What fools we were! The fact that we didn't see a truck driver or a Chinaman should have given us the clue. We glanced around the room and everyone there was staring dolefully at the same sickening dish. Captains at Le Tour D'Argent must have gone through basic training in a used-car lot.

At about this time a rather florid gentleman at the next

table switched his Kiwanis button to "dim," leaned over and extinguished our Crêpes Suzettes with his elbow, and said,

"I see you and the little lady fell for the same line of guff as Mother and I." Mother turned out to be his wife—a rather chic middle-aged lady with blue hair, who was gulping Martinis with the rapacity of a Cossack officer.

"Mother and I," he continued, "have been on a round-the-world cruise on the Kungsholm. It's a lovely ship . . . but I just can't stand smorgasbord."

Why this gentleman who couldn't bear Swedish food decided to spend the better part of a year on the Kungsholm, we never did figure out.

Then, switching his subject sharply, he asked me, "Did you and the little lady ever stand under Victoria Falls with an umbrella? Mother and I did. You must try it some time. And be sure and take along a pint!" At this point he drew out a wallet from which dangled twenty or so gold-plated credit cards. Even Henny, who is known as the fastest credit card in the West, was impressed.

"Nice to know your credit is good all over the world. In the Congo, walked right into a bank—made of mud and twigs. Showed 'em one of these. Walked out with five thousand good American dollars. Mother plunges at Bingo. Where you folks from?" We told him.

"Ah," he said, "well, I own a ranch in Elko. Elko, Nevada. There's a fellow owns a ranch up near me, has something to do with Hollywood. What was his name, Mother?" Mother was too busy working on her magnum of champagne to answer.

"His kids went to school with my boy. Nice youngsters. Let's see . . . there was Dennis, Phillip, Lindsey and Gary. Their father was a real nice neighbor. Used to come over during the holidays. Used to sing 'White Christmas.' Never did find out what line of work he was in."

A half hour later we were walking along the Quai de la Tournelle feeling like a couple on their way to do a Rolaid commercial. Personally, after my treatment in Le Tour D'Argent, I felt like a damn fool—like I did when I was a kid and fell for that gag, "All The Root Beer You Can Drink For Ten Cents." As we walked along the river trying to decide what to do, Henny said,

"Look, sweetie, I know what's on your mind . . . so let's get it over with. I know you're bucking to go to the Lido."

The Lido, as everyone knows, is the Number One tourist attraction in Paris. It's what the Folies Bergère was to the post World War I generation. Regardless of what we say about it here, you will go—but I'll tell you anyway. It is an interminable girly show, no more nude and no less nude than it was in Las Vegas. There are, in addition to the girls, animal acts, Japanese acrobats, Chinese jugglers, colored tap dancers, and Arabian belly dancers. It is sort of a "Brotherhood Week" set to music. Actually to save yourself a lot of money, you can stay home, watch the Ed Sullivan show and pretend the performers and Ed Sullivan haven't got any clothes on.

From here on out we played it by ear. We went from joint to joint and at the Calavados we ran into Martha Hyer and an American writer. It seemed odd to see Martha in Paris. The last time I saw her was on the set of "Ice Palace," the movie we made in Alaska. The four of us joined forces. We covered just about everything. We started at the Scheherazade, which looked like something out of the Arabian nights. It had Cossack-clad waiters gliding around the room bearing flaming swords of goodness-knows-what, and strolling from table to table were about fifty violinists serenading you while you lolled back with your lady love in true archduke fashion. It was all so romantic we were quite carried away, until we were brought up short when we realized that the lead violinist had an American ten dollar bill fanning out from the bridge of the instrument. The French always combine l'amour with business as usual.

We went to the strip joints—Le Crazy Horse, Le Sexy, et al. And in our wanderings we stumbled into Le Monocle, which we found to be the most amusing place in Paris. As Henny later put it, "It's just like any other friendly little neighborhood corner Lesbian joint."

And it was! To say the sexes were confused is putting it mildly. Somehow, though, it had the air of a P.T.A. meeting that had gotten out of hand. The place was owned by a very stern middle-class, middle-aged French lady and her wife. All their nieces, sisters, aunts, cousins and *their* wives helped to wait table, act in the floor show, and play in the band. It was a family affair. In all of Paris we never met such nice sweet, friendly, warm people. They couldn't do enough to make us happy. This was not one of those hoked-up French upholstered sewers. It was actually as Henny described it. They practically never saw a tourist. These were working women. They were lady laborers, taxi drivers, truck drivers, chicken pluckers, plumbers and factory workers. They were very poor and very shabbily dressed in wide-cuffed men's trousers (undoubtedly designed by Khrushchev's tailor), shirts, collars, and ties. They were like working women anywhere who go out of an evening to pick up some broads.

While Frank, Martha's escort, and I were paying the cab, Henny and Martha entered Le Monocle and were greeted by cheers, applause, whistling, stamping and numerous invitations to dance. When we walked in both girls were doing a stately pavan. Henny's partner was dressed like an I.R.T. motorman, complete with patent-leather bow tie. The motorman's name was Gabrielle. She was built like a Sherman tank and had the voice and delivery of a Gallic Marilyn Monroe. The music was supplied by an all "girl-band," and I use the term loosely. It was the most peculiar band I have ever seen. Some of the instruments defied description. Of the ones we could recognize, there were a musical saw, a zither, an under-sized concertina, a cymbal, and believe it or not, a tuba! The musicians were all grandmother types. Each one was over sixty and every one of these sweet beaming grannies was all dressed up in a tuxedo that must have been bought from a stranded Major Bowes unit.

While Henny was dancing she learned that Gabrielle was a taxi driver. Then Henny set about with her high school French and an assist from the "game" to learn a little about the people who were the habitués of Le Monocle.

She asked Gabrielle, "Les hommes ici," she pointed to a trio of males, "sont pederists?"

"Mais oui," answered Gabrielle . . . like "What else?"

"Les autre hommes ici sonts voyeurs?"

"Mais oui," she again replied.

"And who," asked my wife in French, "is that magnificently beautiful girl at the end of the bar?"

"Oh," answered Gabrielle also in French, "he's not a girl . . . he's a homosexual, too."

"I can't believe that," said Henny, "there is nothing unfeminine about him. He's just lovely. Tell you what, Gabrielle, let's get him to dance with my husband. See if you can get him to come over to our table and ask Jimmy for a dance. Only don't say anything to give it away." Gabrielle came back later on an invitation to join us.

Soon a breathless little voice whispered something in French in my ear. I looked up to see the most beautiful dark-eyed, delicate, tiny, feminine looking girl I had seen in all of Paris.

"What does she want?" I asked my wife.

"She's asking you to dance. Why don't you darling?"

When it comes to dancing, a Fred Astaire I am not. When a band stops playing "Little White Lies" in a Meyer Davis tempo, I'm in trouble, but that night it was magic. With that bit of fluff in my arms, I could do no wrong. We opened with a classic "Merry Widow" waltz, featuring the lingering backbend, which we followed with a mad Graustarkian polka, and as a Franco-American salute, we finished with a "Castle Walk." I wondered why my wife and our party were laughing. As we passed by the table I leaned down and whispered,

"Hey, Frank, you ought to dance with this dame. She's dynamite!"

This seemed to convulse them. Then laughingly Frank said, "Jimmy, I hate to tell you this, but the dame in your arms is a guy."

Without missing a beat I told them all, "Well, if that's the case . . . then biologically, this is madness!" And I danced on.

It was a bit of a struggle, but between the five of us we learned from Gabrielle some background on the customers that night. The two who particularly fascinated us were a pair of very young German girls known to the inmates of Le Monocle as Les Bôches. The older and more masculine of the two looked like Hans Brinker. She had flaxen hair, and a Dutch Boy's haircut and was wearing torn, shabby, faded-blue denims and a cap. The younger of the two was, that night, having her eighteenth birthday. She was soft and round and billowy and overly feminine and quite homely. She had popeyes, a slack mouth, and long lank hair-colored hair. She was barefooted and wearing a "for real" peasant blouse and skirt. These two could have won first prize at any masquerade by simply going as the little Dutch Boy and his dyke. It being the petite Deutscher's birthday, everyone was loading her with champagne. So, to really celebrate her natal day, she got up on the floor and did a few bumps. Thinking this was part of the floor show, we applauded. This encouraged her further. She took off her blouse, then her skirt and did a very elaborate grind. We cheered! At last we were seeing the Paris we had heard of. Then as a finish and with great flourish, she peeled off her bra and panties. The stern manageress, who had been busily employed in the kitchen, suddenly came out and saw this Rhine maiden standing in the buff. Then, with all the firmness of a Shaker Heights librarian, started to scream,

"Get out! You are ruining my establishment! You're a disgrace! What will these nice Americans think of my place??? Out, I say!"

She threw the German girl out on the pavement, but neglected to throw her clothes out after her. There was the poor shivering girl in the raw. Just then a drunk staggered by, saw the naked girl lying on the pavement, opened the door and yelled, "Hey, madam . . . your sign fell down!"

Before the floor show started, I thought I'd better order myself some coffee. Since it was getting late I decided on Sanka—so from one of the passing waitresses or waiters, or whatever it was, I said, "S'il vous plaît, voulez-vous donnez-moi une Sanka?"

And she said, "Qu'est-ce que c'est Sanka?"

So I said, "Sanka . . . Sanka . . . coffee. Comprenez-vous?"

"Oui," she smiled. So she returned with "cinq-a" coffee . . . five cups of the stuff!

Now the terrible glaring lights dimmed and there was a fanfare followed by the entrance of the owner who was daintily ringing a huge bronze cow bell. She introduced the first entertainer. As we applauded the entrance of the tough, handsome, blond young man in an open shirt and stove-pipe denim pants, Gabrielle sweetly and patiently explained that *this* one was a female. She sang some sentimental ballads about life in the Paris sewers in a raspy, sexy baritone to hysterical cheers, and bowed off. She was immediately followed by five singers in succession, each exactly like her. Then came the re-appearance of our chatelaine to announce (Gabrielle told us) the Paris debut of a wild seductive belly dancer from Algeria. She told some cockamamie story about how this lovely flower of the desert was really a convent-bred French girl who had been stolen from a nunnery by a fierce shiek and had only recently escaped from his harem. "And," added the chatelaine, "here she is . . . that lovely, desirable, one and only . . . Thelma!", at which point the tuba broke into an untrammeled Arabic version of a Sharallah. Out slithered the seductive Algerian Thelma, looking not unlike Lillian Gish with all the fire and sensuousness of a Zasu Pitts. Her belly dancing suit consisted of a few strings of beads, a yashmak, and a tambourine. She wafted around the floor, did a few gelatinous bumps and a backbend, which, due to the lack of meat on her brisket, caused her to resemble a flesh-colored xylophone.

This concluded her portion of the entrainment. Thelma was not only the stellar attraction of Le Monocle that evening, but was also a glorified door prize. So, due to some mysterious drawing in their co-educational powder room, she was warded to me as my partner for the first dance. My dancing partner spoke not one word of English and had a one-track mind.

We danced for a moment or two and suddenly she stopped, pointed at Henny, and said, "Votre femme est très jolie."

I agreed, "Oui, Oui!"

We danced on. She stopped once again. "L'autre femme

et votre femme sont . . . eh?" she clucked and winked, and I got it.

"No, no, no!" I assured her. We did a little step or two before she stopped me again.

"Votre femme et l'autre femme et vous . . . menage à trois?" I got that one, too.

"Non, non, non!" I told her. She slunk back into my arms and we did another little step. She paused again in deep thought.

Finally she looked up at me and asked, "Vous et l'autre femme sont? . . . eh"

"Look," I told her, "now pay attention! Attendez-vous! L'autre femme! Cinema!" I made like a camera. The eyes and ears of the world.

"Movie star!" I continued, "Martha Hyer!" She looked blankly at me. I could see that I was getting nowhere.

"Me, me," I pointed at myself. "Petit movie star. Cinema . . . Hollywood!!" She shrugged and shook her head.

"Martha Hyer et moi sont dans cinema . . . together." She looked completely blank.

"Le nom de la cinema est 'Ice Palace.'" Nothing!

Desperately I continued, " 'Eecey Palace' Look!" I was frantic. "Maison Glacé!" Still not a thing. "Les Frères Warners"—a complete blank!

I said, "Attendez, Ice Palace . . . Cinema . . . Alaska . . . Alaska, c'est froid! Brrr . . . Brrr . . ."

Somewhere in the dark recesses of her brain two nerve ends crossed and a faint light began to appear.

"Alaska, Alaska," she repeated. Suddenly a bright light glowed. She ran across the room. She stopped at our table and shaking her finger at Martha Hyer, she yelled, "Esquimo!!!"

There is one thing about a trip like ours, it can carry to-getherness a bit too far. Let's face it. You're never apart, not even for a minute. You breakfast together; then you have that conference about how to best spend the day. Then you sightsee together; and you lunch together; and you shop together. Then, because you're tired from all this and there is a big evening to follow, you lie down together; then you dress together; and you dine together; and spend the evening together; and then of course, you come home together. Once in Paris a man wanted to see me about making a picture. How do you think I went to see him? Together! So one morning I had had it.

"I don't know about you," I told Henny, "but I'm going to the barber shop. As a matter of fact I may spend the entire day at the barber shop. Don't try to reach me because I'll be at the barber shop." I expected a wild barrage of "this is the day we go to the Louvre, this is the day we buy the perfume, or this is the day we have lunch at the Eiffel Tower."

Instead she said, "That's fine with me. I'm going to the beauty parlor. I'll be there all day. I'll meet you back here at six o'clock."

The fact that she didn't offer any resistance took some of the wind out of my sails. But off I went to the barber shop, which was located in the basement of the George Cinq Hotel. This was indeed a barber shop! About four attendants helped you out of your coat and, as soon as you were comfortable, a bartender from the barber shop's own private bar came in to take your order. My barber was charm itself. He was immaculate in his striped trousers and a smock. Fortunately, he spoke a bit of English. He ushered me to the chair and before I knew it he had me horizontal, and just before he put me under a mountain of aromatic towels, I caught a glimpse of three or four manicurists in black leotards and long black tights hovering around me. From my relaxed position under the mount of perfume and steam, I felt one of my hands being gently put into a bowl of warm water, but not before it had been reassuringly squeezed. The next thing I felt was a gentle tug on my shoe. I muttered something about wanting a shine. Then I felt my shoe being removed. I thought to myself, "Damn clever, these French! They take your shoes off to shine them."

Next came the sock. This was getting out of hand. I didn't come in to get my feet shined. When I felt my feet being immersed in a bucket of water, I pulled off the towels and sat bolt upright. It was then that I realized that I was getting a pedicure. I was getting a pedicure by one of those mesh-clad dryads—with a reassuring pat on the big toe. (Note: To foreign powers—if ever I have access to the secret files containing the information you wish to extract, don't waste your time with the brainwashing or the threats to my loved ones. Just give me a pedicure. I'll talk! Talk? I'll drive you to Oak Ridge!! I'll pay your expenses at Cape Canaveral!!!)

Now my elegant barber sat me up, took off the towels and took a bow. By instinct I bowed back. On my left was a chick giving me a manicure. At my feet was the chiropodist, giving me my pedicure (in France only a chiropodist is allowed to give pedicures). She was putting soft cotton between my toes. I was beginning to like the pedicure. I even liked the color—"Butterfly Pink." This girl had the wildest hairdo. It was all cut off in points like an artichoke. She looked like a Medieval idiot.

I said, "Votre coiffeur est très chic."

"It is very kookie, non? Très rookine, n'est-ce pas?"

I agreed. I gathered that rookine is French for kookie. Then to make conversation, I said, "You know, this is my first pedicure. I never got one back home in Hollywood."

She looked up. "Hollywood? You know Marilyn Monroe?"

"Yes," I told her. "I made a picture with her in 1951." I assured her that Marilyn was a lovely girl.

The manicurist joined in. "You live in Beverly Hills?"

"No," I said, "I live in a place called Bel Air." She was crestfallen. She had only heard of Beverly Hills.

"Beverly Hills is very clean community," she said, obviously repeating something she had read in an American movie magazine.

I said, with all the civic pride in me rising to the fore, "Bel Air is even cleaner. As you enter Bel Air there's a sign that says:

PIGEONS FLYING OVER HERE MUST FLY UP-SIDE DOWN!" They all pretended, at least, to get the joke, and the shop rocked with laughter.

She said, "You 'ave nice house?"

"Nice house?" "We've got two swimming pools, HIS . . . and HERS." They screamed at this one.

I continued, "My house is beautifully furnished, too. Why the rug in my living room is so thick, that sometimes a hat goes across it and we never know who is under it until it reaches the tiled floor in the hall." They roared. Without realizing it, I was doing part of my act.

"You know," said the pedicurist, "you remind me of another American . . . Milton Byerle."

"Who," I asked. "Oh, Milton Berle. Well, thank you!" I was flattered.

She continued, "Milton Byerle, we say here, est un cabotin." Now I was really flattered.

"Oh," I said, "is that so?" "What is a cabotin?"

"A cabotin is a loud-mouthed ham!!!" said a voice from behind the partition.

"Wait a minute," I yelled, "What kind of an insult . . ." Then I realized. It was the voice of my everlovin' wife. Was there no escaping her? The French, they are a clever race. Even their beauty parlors are co-educational. And the worst part of it was when I paid for my haircut, shave, manicure, pedicure and shine, they had also added Henny's shampoo, rinse, wave comb-out, facial—and—four Daiquiris? Now I know what they mean when they say, "I went to the barber shop and got the works!"

One of the most amazing sights in Paris is the American drugstore. It is on the Champs Élysées up a ways from the Avenue George Cinq and almost to the Arc de Triomphe. I'm sorry but when it comes to giving directions in Paris, that's the best I can do. It opened while we were there and was the season's big attraction. The Parisiennes flocked to see that amazing emporium. It had electric eyes that opened the doors automatically. It had garish yellow walls and ceilings which were bathed in the kind of neon light that, if you have someone at the correct angle, makes it possible to see his bridgework through his cheek. It sold all the assorted trash that they dispense in the drugstores back home. There were the same silly departments that have nothing whatever to do with drugs, plus two "Photomaton" machines that you could not possibly get near. There were three lines of people in front of them day and night waiting to get their pictures taken and their X-rays retouched.

One afternoon we were sitting with Art Buchwald at the California bar, which is an American newspaperman's hangout and conveniently located across the street from the Herald Tribune. We were talking about the behavior pattern of Americans in Paris. We all agreed that the tourist is a lonely man. He seeks out the companionship of people he would never in a million years have anything to do with at home. All he wants to do is talk about his trip. The terrible thing is that the people he seeks out want to talk about *their* trip. Some of our observations he put in his column.

NEW YORK
April 23   HERALD TRIBUNE

ART BUCHWALD
TOURIST TOPPING

One of the great sports played during the spring and summer months in Europe is tourist topping. Any number can play, and the object of the game is to top another tourist no matter what the opponent says. Mr. Jim Backus, the American television comedian and the voice of Magoo, the famed animated cartoon character, claims he's been playing the game since he arrived in Europe and he hasn't won yet. Part of tourist topping, Mr. Backus explained, was to make the other party think that no matter where you are, it's nothing compared to where he has just come from.

"When we were in London we met tourists who said it was nothing compared to Paris. Now that we're in Paris everyone says it's nothing compared to Rome. I'm sure when we get to Rome people will say it's nothing compared to London.

"One of the major strategies of a tourist topper is to make sure his opponent isn't having a good time.

"Even my wife has been topping me on this trip. Last week I took a walk alone and when I got back to the hotel I said to her: 'Guess who I saw on the Champs-Élysées today! Ingrid Bergman!' She said: 'That's nothing. I went over to the Galeries Lafayette to buy some gifts this morning and bumped into Nina Khrushchev.'"

The last night we were in Paris we had had the rich food. We were so sick of Crêpes Suzettes and Pot au Crème and Le Poulet Farci en Côcotte and Confits D'oie and Bécasses flambées and Côtes de Porc la Charcutiere, and those fish, staring up at you balefully. Through a bit of luck we found sanctuary in a delightful Kosher deli-catessen called "Chez Louis." Oh, for a nice simple dish of Chicken in the Pot . . . and it was wonderful! The side dishes of sauerkraut and dill pickles. The pink horse-radish and the cheese cake and the tea in the glass. Even the waiter was "Chez Louis'" answer to the "Stage Deli-catessen."

When we asked him what time it was, he replied, "Pardon, ce n'est pas mon table."

Somehow we felt we had never left home!

CHAPTER 10

what are you doing after the orgy?

THIS IS Henny——

London, as we know, is traditionally a man's town. And though Paris is essentially feminine, it, too, is best described by a male. For who better than a man can describe a beautiful woman. But Rome—that's a different story. Rome is for girls—and I have the black and blue marks to prove it. Let's take it from the top!

The Paris-to-Rome express was sort of an "instant Super Chief." Unlike its American counterpart, there was none of that nonsense of starting off at a glide, coming to a stop in the yards, picking up mail, stopping at a suburb and finally, half an hour later, really getting under way. This train took off like a scalded dog!

There is no such thing as a porter in a crisp white coat standing at the end of each car with his footstool, waiting to help you climb aboard. In Europe the trains are on a level with the station platform, and the porters, such as they are, were huddled inside the trains on their haunches, smoking dark brown do-it-yourself cigarettes. These porters regarded all passengers with suspicion—as though they had boarded the train for the sole purpose of blowing it up, or at least filching one of their Limoges potties.

Let us suppose that the train was to leave at 3:04. Straight up, after the last three goats had been tucked aboard, a man in a Schubert musical comedy uniform, blew a shrill whistle and ready-or-not, all the doors sklonked shut. And off we went! By the time it reached the end of the platform, it was going as fast as it would go for the rest of the trip.

We never did find out who the train belonged to. Was it privately owned? Was it jointly owned by Italy and France? Nobody, neither the French staff on the French side nor the Italian staff who took over when we crossed the border, seemed to know . . . and what's more nobody cared. It gave us the feeling that we were traveling in limbo.

Later, in the diner, we were studying the menu—not because we had any choice—but to see in advance what they had decided to give us to eat. Much to our amazement we found that they thought it fitting to serve:

> Cream of Tomato Soup
> Broiled Chicken
> Mashed Potatoes
> Peas
> Vanila Ice Cream
> American Coffee

As we looked at this "Chamber of Commerce special" with utter disgust, a waiter, staggering under the weight of his tray, reeled by. On it was a casserole full of some succulent dish made of sausage and beans, plus a loaf of hot French bred, the aroma of which drove us out of our minds, and a bottle of wine.

Without a moment's hesitation, Jimmy said to the waiter, "We will have two of that!"

"Non, monsieur!" he told him. "That is not for such as you! That is for Monsieur le Conducteur et Monsieur l'Engineer. You are veree luckee! You are getting the oh so beauteefool American dinnair. You are an American, non?"

"I am an American, yes!" said Jim. "But bring Mrs. Benedict Arnold and me the 'Caboose Special.' "

After the delicious dinner which the engineer had so graciously shared with us, Jim summoned the waiter and told him he wanted to send the kind engineer a bottle of wine with our compliments.

"Non, monsieur," said the waiter, "some othair time, perhaps. I am afraid Monsieur L'Engineer has had too much already." With this reassuring thought we retired for the night.

From the moment you enter Italy, you are aware that you are a woman. Everybody is busy giving you the hot eye—I mean everybody—and in a group. They do group flirting. They stare at you. They roll their eyes. They do heavy breathing and sighing. Their nostrils flare and they behave like silent movie actors. It's corny . . . but it's wonderful! And then, of course, they do quite a bit of jostling. This, too, is a group effort. When they see you approach along the too narrow sidewalk, they start a flirtatious game of pushing and shoving each other, at the same time never taking their eyes off you and loudly describing your charm to one another with much sighing and "kissy" noises. You try to ignore them as you aloofly walk by, but they manage to give you a little nudge and a push here and there. Once in a while one of them gets up nerve enough to pinch . . . and when he does the others are so ecstatic they push and shove each other harder than before. The pincher, of course, is a momentary hero! The flirting goes on all day long, wherever you are and whatever you do. The room clerk gives you the key and murmurs little Italian nothings in your ear, all the while holding your hand. The doorman instead of helping you out of the cab by your elbow, helps you out of the cab by your thigh. They call out after you wherever you go, "Bella ragazza," if you're a girl, or "Bell' uomo," if you are an indeterminate.

They holler endearments in Italian, and to show you that they "dig," they yell in broken English: "Where-a y' staying? Whatsa ya phona numba?" And, "Hey, Americana!"

I was livid. Here I was walking along the street minding my own business! I never was so insulted in all my life. How dare they call me an American!!! Some of them did think I was an Italian, though. Why not! I could say: "Avanti," and "Benissimo," and "Pronto," and "Grazie," and "Un bello brutto uomo."

The winking, the rolling eyes, the sighs, the flaring nostrils . . . all of it went on . . . even when your husband was present. But they are such masters, their timing was so sure, that Jimmy never once caught on.

I never take elevators. To me they're vertical airplanes . . . and I would rather walk (I used to do a daily radio show on the twenty-second floor of CBS, so I'm a pretty good stair climber). We were on the sixth floor of the Excelsior Hotel. I always walked down. I would have preferred to walk up too, but I never got the chance. Some gorgeous blackeyed, lavishly uniformed employee (I never could figure out what they were in that hotel), would grab my elbow (I was lucky), and firmly march me to the elevator where a breathtakingly beautiful Roman elevator operator (they must cast these guys at Cinecittà) would take over the operation and park me inside his wrought-iron basket on a string. I could never make my

point with either of them. How could I tell them I was
afraid of elevators? How could I explain in Italian that
I was some kind of a nut?

Then the handsome one would come to a complete stop
between floors, take his hands off the lever (this would
make me shudder, not at the thought of what he might
do to me, but because I have always had the feeling that
if you ever let go of that lever, the elevator would go right
down to the bottom of the shaft), and then he would
simply lean against the wall, arms akimbo, and stare at
me and cluck! When the ringing of the elevator bell got
really persistent, he would reluctantly start the thing up
again. I never did get the message. I still can't figure out
what he was building. After the European trip was over,
I confessed it all to Jimmy:

". . . and then he would stop the damn thing right between floors while I was so scared I was shaking all over!
And then he would just lean back and stare at me with
those big soft brown eyes! And then he would just smile
and cluck!"

And Jimmy said: "He would do that to you? Well . . .
what do you think he did to me!!!"

One day I frantically called my beautiful, witty friend,
Mary Chamberlain, who has been living in Rome for six
or seven years. She wrote a delightful and most informa-
tive book about that city and its people called, *Dear
Friends and Darling Romans*. Since she loved and understood them so well, I knew she could help me.

"Mary," I said, "today they did it again . . . only this
time you'll never believe it, they couldn't have been over
eleven or twelve years old . . . and they did all those
same things to me! All that pushing and shoving and
jostling and grabbing! . . . the same tricks! . . . and
they're just babies!! They yelled things I didn't understand
and asked for my room number . . . and where I was

staying . . . and, oh you know, Mary. And I was so shocked. I don't get it!"

And Mary said, "Don't worry about it, darling, just smile at them and when you are safely out of their way, give them a little wink to encourage them."

I was horrified!! "Mary," I screamed, "what do you mean encourage them? Why would I do that?"

"Because, Henny love," she told me, "they need it . . . they're practicing!"

Thanks to Mary, who is a bit of a social leader, we met some of the upper crust Roman society, plus the "Dolce Vita" set. They were all charming and very kind. Did we care to have the car and chauffeur for the day? Would we like them to drive us to Naples? Would your husband mind if I took you to Fontana tomorrow afternoon to shop? After a week or so of this it struck us . . . we had never once met a wife. These charming men were all happily married and made no bones about it. But when you asked the whereabouts of their wives, they would look ever so sad for a moment, cast their lovely Latin eyes skyward and say: "Unfortunately my wife is at the seashore," or "Due to a respiratory ailment, my wife is in the mountains," or "Due to a bereavement, my wife is in the North."

Pretty cool, these Romans. If you will notice, they never gave the exact location of where the wife was . . . just a sort of general geographical description. They never said: "My wife is in Florence . . . or Venice . . . or Milano." Nothing that definite! Can you imagine an American on the loose, saying: "Unfortunately my wife is somewhere in the Great Lakes area," or "Due to a respiratory ailment, my wife is in the Rocky Mountains," or "Due to a bereavement, my wife is in the Mississippi basin." At best an American man, when trapped, makes a feeble joke like: "I have the best wife in the country . . . and I wish she'd stay there!"

Jimmy had a very interesting observation for me one night. He said he has found that in hotels in America, men are apt to nail him in the lobby and say: "I hope you have a minute. My wife would love to meet you and get your autograph for our little girl. I'm waiting for her and she'll be right down."

In Europe, for some unknown reason, the situation was reversed. The women were always in the lobby waiting for the men. Jimmy was constantly button-holed by lady tourists. One night when Jimmy was waiting for me in the lobby he was soon surrounded by a group of them who wanted his autograph.

"For my little boy, of course!"

"It's for my niece, you know!"

"My neighbor's daughter will be so thrilled!" Grownups, you know, never want your autograph for themselves. It's always for some poor innocent child. As he was handing back a pencil, a hand reached out and firmly steered him away from the purple orchid and flower hat set, to a post behind a giant rubber plant. This lady was in direct contrast to the others. She was full of free-flowing uncontrolled curves, which were clearly visible through her Italian knit sheath, which I might add, had a decolletage down to her kneecaps. Her eyes were outlined in thick black crayon and, on her pale lips, she wore an inviting smile. As she teetered on her five-inch patent-leather heels, Jimmy thought he detected a buzzing sound in her beehive coiffeur.

Somewhat at a loss, Jimmy said: "Would you like my autograph?"

"I woulda lika you autographa ona Banka America Exapressa."

Still at a loss, Jim said: "I don't get it."

So she made sure that he did!

"You getta it, babee," she said as she undulated her hips insinuatingly. "You comma weetha mia anda youa getta it. We spenda nica eveneeng . . . anda you getta it. Joosta geeva me feeftee Americano dollaires, non?"

Jim, who's been around, knowing an insult would be the best way to get rid of her, said:

"Fifty dollars! . . . I'll give you FIVE!!!" She did what we in show business call a "rave off." She spat. She made the Sicilian sign of the horns. She hissed and screamed and called down on his head curses that went back to Romulus and Remus. About fifteen minutes later when Jim and I were seated at the Excelsior bar, the same lady, still on the prowl, sashayed into the room, spotted me sitting with Jim, stalked over, pointed her finger at me and in a voice of thunder announced:

"See whata you getta for fiva dollaires!!!"

You always hear arguments pro and con about which city and country have the most beautiful women. Well, I'm sick of those arguments, and anyway who cares. Let me tell you which city has the handsomest men! Rome!!! And the best of these are the police. And the best looking of all the police are the dashing "carabinieri" in their wild blue capes. Rome seems to be full of police . . . and indeed it is . . . as they have six different kinds of officers of the law. They tell me that there are more police, nuns, and priests in Rome than private citizens. I never saw so many priests and nuns.

I remember telling that to Jimmy who said: "Why not . . . this is the home office."

Once in the drugstore I was remarking about the charm of the Italian male to the lady pharmacist when an aristocratic looking woman standing next to me, who was having her ring refilled, said: "My dear, if you really want to see our handsomest men, you should travel on one of our

Italian liners where they are hand picked for their masculinity, their beauty and charm." I tried to persuade Jimmy to let us return home on the Leonardo da Vinci, but he wasn't buying it.

"Italian ships are too dangerous. The captain never knows whether to use the oil for fuel or salad dressing." (Jimmy always strikes back with a bad joke. Just for that I'm having him barred from the "Playboy Club.")

To me, Rome was enchantment. To Jim, Rome was one single block—that block which runs down the whole street in front of the Excelsior Hotel and houses "Doney's" sidewalk cafe. Doney's is a theatrical hangout—an open-air Sardi's. But to Jim, Doney's was a home away from home. He would be there for breakfast, drink innumerable cups of coffee with pals who were in Rome making pictures. Then he would have lunch which lasted for three or four hours. This was all so exhausting that he would have to go upstairs and take a nap so he would be refreshed for the Doney's cocktail hour, the Doney's dinner, the after-dinner coffees, the snack, the late snack, then more friends, the late shift and the 2:00 A.M. nightcap—and so to bed.

By the second day he was a regular and had his own table next to a hydrant so that friends with dogs could discuss things without interruption. By the end of a week he was an institution, a landmark, a one-man block party . . . and I wasn't speaking to him! Finally I blew my top! I walked up to my husband who was sitting in the blazing noonday Roman sun, reading a two-week old copy of *Variety*.

"Listen, Buster, that's all. Cut!! We came all this way to see Rome, and not read Variety and not see a lot of hams you see too much of at home anyway. And now . . . march! Into this car I rented! We're going to St. Peters!"

"St. Peters," my spouse screamed, "I can't! Bruce Cabot, Buster Crabbe, and the 'Bowery Boys' are coming here for lunch."

"On your feet," I snarled through clenched teeth. "We are going to St. Peters basilica, even though it means that I don't go to Elizabeth Arden's all afternoon!"

No one had ever prepared me for the beauty, the vastness, the utterly breathtaking magnificence of St. Peters. Its splendor even got through to some teenage kids standing next to us. One of them paid it the highest compliment he was capable of.

"Gee," he sighed, "this is sure the Marilyn Monroe of churches."

Jimmy was quiet and reverent, and very very thrilled. He didn't even miss Doney's.

"It's just magnificent," he whispered. "The whole thing is so breathtaking—the paintings, the sculpture . . . and those mosaics. Look, honey, look! Even the phone booths are made of solid mahogany."

"Phone booths . . . you Cleveland plowboy! Those are confessionals!"

We went outside later and wandered about the magnificent St. Peter's square. Above and to the right is the Pope's window at which he sometimes appears, and on this day of all days we were very lucky. What impressed us was the deep affection the Italians seem to have for their new Pope. We had always assumed that there would be an awed hush upon the appearance of his holiness. They told us there used to be with Pope Pius, but for this new Pope, who came from the people, a cheer went up and then calls of "Hello, John." Kisses were thrown and it was altogether a demonstration of very warm affection. We later learned that the Pope loves to wander around the streets of Rome alone. He had been in the habit of sneaking out of the Vatican to take walks and was affectionately nicknamed "Johnnie Walker." But now they have two motorcycle police at the Vatican twenty-four hours a day to guard him.

I asked Jimmy if he knew an appropriate joke to help me tie up this paragraph and "put a ribbon on it," as they say on Madison Avenue. So he gave me one, and I said: "Darling, I can't use that. It's been kicked around for years." Well, oddly enough, the other night we went to see "The Hostage," and it rocked the house. That same old joke! Believe me, it literally stopped the show. We are constantly stunned by our so-called hep theater friends and their deep appreciation of old radio jokes . . . but maybe they're right. So here goes! If you're ever in Rome, you can easily reach the Pope . . . his phone number is Vat 69!

One day Jimmy decided to rent a car so that we could get out of the city. He was having breakfast, need I say where, and when I joined him he was sitting with a new-found friend. His companion was one of those gentlemen who instead of rising to acknowledge his introduction to a lady, simply leans back further and looks her up and down. His horizontal chum was named Philladorrio Feffi. If you dig the type, he was the best-looking professional dreamboat on the Via Veneto. The easiest way to describe him is to say he was a male Elizabeth Taylor and with just as much cleavage. His shirt V'd open to his slim waist, where it was gathered into a large knot. His hairless body gleamed directly in the sunlight and, like the rest of his ilk, he was probably shaved from head to foot (which is more than I can say for his girl friends). Unlike most Italians, he was obviously quite tall, since his legs covered the three remaining chairs. His pants were so tight I know he had to take Novocaine to get into them, unless of course, they were painted on. And I could hardly wait to see him stand up in his tight pointed shoes—they looked like they were a continuation of his pants. His head was thickly covered with blue-black ringlets, which seemed to have just been sprayed with dew. He had a full set of curly bangs dancing across his forehead. I had a feeling he was hiding something under them—maybe a hideous scar or possibly he was branded. Every extension of his body that I could see was covered with jewelry. There were rings, bracelets, charms, medallions and on one ankle a massive slave bracelet . . . complete with chain. I was tempted to ask him if by any chance he pulled second oar with Ben Hur and was this his day off from the galley? Come to think of it, he must have had a hell of a time sneaking out of a bedroom with all of that clanking. Suddenly he spoke—and in pretty good English. In about five minutes I learned from Signore Feffi that he came from a distinguished family, that he had a title which he deigned to use, that he was a soldier of fortune, a dress designer, a one-time member of the underground, a Grand Prix winner . . . and could have any woman he wanted. He added that he was now trying to decide whether or not to become a movie star, while I was trying to decide whether or not to tell him to get lost. That decision was taken out of my hands when the love of my life piped up.

"Guess what! We don't have to rent a car! Feffi has a friend who happens to have a limousine and he is going to let us have it for the day. And my friend, Feffi, here, is going along as guide just for fun!"

"Guide!" I was amazed. "Him?"

I thought of a guide as a somewhat different breed . . . more like a learned cab driver . . . not this big slumberous over-ripe plum! Feffi turned to me and for the first time really opened his eyes:

"You see, Signora Backus, while I was a political prisoner and my mother the Principessa's Ethiopian plantations were being confiscated, I had to earn a living. So, due to my vast store of knowledge, what is more natural than I be a guide, non?"

"Well, thanks a lot," I told him, "but we don't need a guide. We're just going to get in a car and I'm going to drive us through the Italian countryside and on up to. . . ."

"Just a minute, Henny! Not so fast! You're never going to get behind a wheel in this crazy country. These people aren't drivers! They're Kamikazes! I don't want to hear you even suggest that you're going to drive. The answer is absolutely NO! Now, listen to me, baby. I don't actually want to drive either; so why don't we get a nice professional chauffeur like Signore Feffi's friend. They know the country and they can take us up to Tivoli to see the d'Este Villa and those fountains you keep talking about."

"What a coincidence!" shouted Feffi, slithering up on his pointy feet. "The d'Este Villa once belonged to our family. I am a d'Este on my mother's side. That palace and those thousand fountains were ours. That is why my Italian family is so impoverished. What a water bill!!!"

By this time he had steered us into a limousine which just happened to be parked at the curb beside our table. Before we were actually seated in the car he mumbled something to his friend, the driver, in Italian, and off we zoomed zigzagging jerkily down the street through all that traffic. Now, for openers, this was not the ideal automobile for sight-seeing. It was a vintage Cadillac sedan. It looked like a getaway car from "The Untouchables." It was of the period when those cars had rounded black leather rears with no windows. Just grand for sight-seeing! From both of the jump seats (one for his legs, of course), where he commanded a perfect view of the passing scenery, Philladorrio Feffi, loving the role of guide gave it all he had.

"This pyramid we are now passing is the funeral monument of Magistrate Caius Cestius. He died in 43 B. C. Behind it lies the Protestant cemetery."

Big deal! As he orated so grandly, I was reading the same thing word for word in the guide book on my lap. When Signore Feffi turned again to see where we were, I hissed in Jim's ear, "I don't know about you . . . but I can't see a damn thing. Alan Shepard had better visibility than we've got."

"Quiet, dear," Jim whispered, "He'll hear you!"

"What do you mean, hear me . . . with that Charlotte Bronte bun over each ear?"

Feffi droned on with much emotion and many gestures.

"We are now going through the biggest park in Rome, the Borghese, with its own art galleries."

I followed him with my guide book. I had to hand it to him. He learned it word for word.

"Over there," he continued, "is the Giardino d'el Lago, which you have heard is. . . ."

I poked Jim in the ribs. "Would you mind asking Mr. Feffi if he has a periscope, dear boy! I hope you're not thinking of paying this bejeweled Latin Lowell Thomas one red cent for this ill fated junket."

"Will you stop it, Henny! You don't pay a man like this. You just give him a token of appreciation . . . like fifty dollars at the end of the day—if he'll take it."

"If he'll take it," I snorted, "and what will you pay broken-nosed Luigi in the front there with the hand-painted tie, who is driving this hearse?"

"I'm only giving him fifteen dollars!" I didn't even answer him—and besides Feffi was getting so carried away with his oratory, I was becoming fascinated.

"We are now parallel with the old Appian Way," he boomed with gestures. "It was built nearly twenty-three centuries ago to join Rome and Capua. The road is lined with ancient Roman graves, for in those days it was forbidden to bury people in the city itself. Everywhere you see the inscription S. P. Q. R., which stands for SENATUS POPULUSQUE ROMANUS, "The Roman Senate and People."

I was beside myself! Sixty-five dollars a day—for what! For the privilege of sitting in this hot leather closet.

"It's so dark in here, I can't even see you, thank God! Oh well, maybe I can read all about it in book form when I'm sitting in my nice cool cell doing five to ten for hitting you over the head with Signore Feffi!"

Poor Jimmy was chagrined for a moment. "I'm sorry," he said, "if you can't see from back here, I'll tell you what —I'll have him stop the car and you can sit up front with the driver."

"There isn't room, dear," I replied. "Perhaps you didn't notice when we got into this Mafia boxcar, but there are a number of other passengers in front. There are two nice big buckets of live eels and a crate of squid. I think your friends are running a hot delivery service on the side. And from the way this car smells, I think we're sitting on the live bait tank."

Two hours later we arrived at the Villa d'Este, Feffi's ancestral summer cottage with its thousand fountains. Built in the sixteenth century, the villa was a showplace of its day with the finest gardens of the Renaissance which contained those fabulous fountains of every size, shape and description, the flow of whose water could be regulated by stepping on certain stones in the courtyard. Feffi whisked us from room to room with a running commentary.

The rooms in the Villa d'Este were bare and bleak and dark and dank, and completely devoid of furniture. All that was to be seen were some barely discernible ancient murals and frescoes, a few that had been restored, and one or two pieces of sculpture. We went up a flight of stairs and saw one room. Then down a few steps to a suite. Then round and round a towering stairway to a great hall. Then up a step to a ballroom, and then down three steps to a salon. Practically every room was on a different elevation. It was a great place to visit in the daytime, but I would hate to have to spend the night there. It was so clammy, it reminded me of a split-level bath house. I sort of expected an attendant to hand me one of those giant locker keys that dangle from your wrist by a thick rubber band.

Feffi's narration carried on throughout the tour of the Villa. He rambled on like an overheated Expresso machine. He was so slick he almost sounded like he knew what he was talking about.

"This magnificent fresco," he steamed, "was painted by Fra Angelico, that pious Dominican monk, who was one of the inspired men of the Renaissance. He executed this commission at the request of my ancestor, Cardinal Ippolito d'Este the Younger, right after he finished his great work on the private chapel in the Vatican, which as we all know was done at the personal request of Pope Nicholas V."

Well! Inasmuch as Fra Angelico died in 1455 and the d'Este Villa was built in 1549, that was a very interesting piece of information Mr. Feffi was giving us. I decided to file it away for future reference, like when Mr. Feffi was through for the day and it was time to reward him. He shepherded us into the next salon. Then, with eyes half closed and in a semi-hypnotic trance, he continued as he pointed somewhat vaguely at the walls.

"This fine fresco is a study of light and color as a means of giving depth and solidity to the forms within the picture, painted by Masolina d'a Panicale and his pupil, Masaccio. It presents a vivid contrast to the piety of Fra Angelico." I stared at the fresco and let Mr. Feffi hang himself.

"Note the technique, tempera, in which dry colors ground very fine were moistened and held together with a binding medium of glue, usually the white of egg."

Feffi had broken the time barrier. Without being aware of it, he had gone from the fifteenth century to the 1920s and was inaccurately describing a buckling mural on the wall of the d'Este Villa that had been painted by Mussolini's equivalent of the W. P. A. By the time he opened his great big larcenous eyes, it was too late.

This mural of happy farmers and their tractors would have been equally at home in any post office in Missouri, except for one jarring note, a biplane piloted by a blue jowled aviator who bore a striking resemblance to Il Duce himself, who, instead of dropping bombs on the countryside was showering it with an antipasto of flowers.

A half hour later, as I drove along the beautiful countryside humming to myself and admiring the gnarled old olive trees from my large front window, a final thought suddenly came to me. I turned a bit toward the rear seat where Jimmy was sitting on the live bait tank between Signore Feffi and the driver with the handpainted tie, with his feet in the buckets of live eels and the crate of squid in his lap.

". . . and furthermore, Jimmy, tell Mr. Feffi he has to pay for the gas!"

As a word of warning, watch out for the guides! Some of them aren't! Beware of the sharp young men with the pointy toes who hang around the Via Veneto and the Spanish steps and tell you they have a friend who happens to own a limousine. Don't you believe it! It's just a car they've rented on speculation for the express purpose of giving you a garbled guided tour for as much as they can get out of it. They spend long hours in the sunshine, flashing their new silver cigarette cases at each other, and bragging about the rich American ladies with whom they scored last night. It's tough to cope with these characters. They're very sly and disarmingly charming. Once in Mexico when I left Jimmy alone to buy some baskets and huaraches and some watered-down Chanel No. 5, he unbalanced a guide who suggested an illicit rendezvous with his sister.

Jimmy said:

"Go out with your sister . . . I can't even drink your water!"

The next morning, entirely Feffiless, we set off to see the Forum. Quite frankly we hadn't been to bed. We set off at dawn to see the sun come up over the Forum. The impact of it was stunning. It really rocked us! In the eerie morning light, the columns, surrounded by mist, seemed to have their capitols in the sky. As the sun came up we saw the little temples, the tall green grass, and the hundreds of cats that inhabit the place. Right there it all started, over 2,700 years ago, there on the hill called the Palatine. There was the Forum Romanum where Mark Antony mourned the body of Julius Caesar—and then in the distance—we could hardly believe our ears—we heard:

"Friends, Romans, Countrymen . . . lend me your ears!"

"I don't know about you," said Jimmy, "but I'm hearing things. This going without sleep! I had better go back to the hotel and lie down . . ."

"Look! Look, Jimmy! Just look!!"

Then from behind a memorial column slowly emerged a figure in a toga, with an olive wreath around his head.

"Jim," I said, "if this is some terrible joke you're playing on me . . . like if you've gotten hold of that Leon Schwab someplace and are . . ."

"Leon Schwab! Honey, if you think I'd joke about a thing like this . . . hey, wait a minute! Do you know who that is? It's Peter Ustinov! What's he doing here . . .

and at this hour of the morning . . . and dressed like that!"

We ran to see. We stopped running when we realized he must be shooting a picture—but which one? When it comes to playing Romans, Peter, since his Academy Award winning performance in "Spartacus," to say nothing of his "Nero" in "Quo Vadis," was the noblest Roman of them all. As luck would have it, he was working with Jim's old gang, the "Dave Garroway show." Jim had substituted for Dave for the past two years whenever the early bird star went on his vacations, and I had been on the show too. So we were all very glad to see each other. They were in the Forum by the dawn's early light, because as a rule that is when your day starts on location. They were doing a number of segments of the "Today" show in Rome to be broadcast in the United States. But as happy as we were to see them, somehow it detracted from our little foray into Roman antiquity to be seated on that step where Brutus perhaps made his impassioned speech to the citizens of Rome, eating a box lunch complete with hard-boiled eggs and tangerines, watching a man with a sponge applying body make-up to a local college athlete playing a centurion. It was exactly what we had come all the way from Hollywood to get away from. Madison Avenue, Vine Street, and the Appian Way had all become one. We began to giggle. We were reminded of the time Jim spent six months in a centurion suit when he did the movie version of George Bernard Shaw's "Androcles and the Lion", which I am sure you have all seen on the late, late, late show. It was produced by Howard Hughes, old tennis shoes himself, cost $5,000,-000, and was a colossal flop. But then he never could get anything off the ground!

In this picture Jim played a centurion which is the Roman version of a top sergeant—sort of a Stone Age

William Bendix. It was an especially tough picture because he was expected in "Make-up" every morning at six, to get his hair curled. This made me very happy. At last he was getting a taste of what we girls go through—having our hair done every single morning and having to get into the make-up department at least an hour before the men. Nowadays, unless it is a character part or a costume picture, the only make-up an actor uses is a fast spongeful of pancake. But not this time! In addition to the ringlet job with a hot curling iron that terrified him, it took a full hour and three wardrobe men to get him into the authentic Roman armor he wore. This was no fun-in-the-parlor costume. It was for real! They had a professor from U.C.L.A. to check it daily. This professor is now in the Kennedy cabinet.

Get this outfit! First he got into his part-the-feet-in-the-middle sandals with the leather thongs that wrapped around the legs up to the knees. Then came a suede night-shirt, followed by a skirt made of long heavy leather straps studded with chunks of iron, under which he wore flesh-colored panties for obvious reasons. Over this went a chemise made of steel chains. This was gathered in by a belt from which hung two tremendous jeweled swords. There was a June Allyson collar made of chains and medals from which hung a fifteen-foot red plush "Loew's Pitkin" curtain. On both arms he wore classical butcher's cuffs of cowhide in which were stashed two daggers. To top all this off, there was a helmet with a crazy pony tail down the back. When they first put this helmet on Jim, it was so heavy he blacked out, so they had to line it with sponge rubber to prevent a concussion. For accessories, he had a gnarled club in his left hand and a spear in his right. Because parts of his body were exposed, he had to be shaved and covered with body make-up, which was applied with an ice cold sponge at 7:00 A. M.

This outfit was so cumbersome and heavy that he actually had to be helped down every single step by two men. Jimmy told me he learned by the second day that to think of going to the men's room in that rig was sheer madness! He was grounded in that department till he was pushed and pulled back to his dressing room at the end of the day. They say the Roman soldiers raped and pillaged their way across Europe. Pillaged, yes . . . but . . . unless they were invading a patient nation!!! And as for winning any battles, the enemy must have known far in advance that they were being snuck up on, for dressed like this in this airtight regalia, the Roman army must certainly have risked offending.

Hollywood and its business of making motion pictures once more loused up an otherwise perfect Roman holiday. On another occasion Jimmy and I went to the Colosseum to try to recapture the glory that was Rome when we were jerked out of our reverie by Jack Palance, who appeared from behind one of the bleachers carrying a sword, trident, and net, and done up in a fur bikini. He was shooting some celluloid gem that I think was called, "I was a Teenaged Attila the Hun." The director wasn't helping our mood any either. He was days behind on this movie, which was using locations all over Rome. His explanation for taking so long was a simple one. "Rome," he told us "wasn't shot in a day!"

When we were in Rome, and according to *Variety* things haven't changed a bit, the town was invaded by motion picture companies from all over the world, to say nothing of the Italian film industry all making pseudo-historical costume pictures with plenty of sex—known in the trade as "Bra and Sand" pictures. We went out to Cinecitta studios to visit some friends. A very interesting fact that the Italian technique of making movies is that they shoot them exactly like silent movies. The actors, all from different parts of the world, speak their lines in their native tongues. For example, the company we saw that day had a leading man who was English, who spoke his lines in English. The leading lady was Italian. She spoke hers in Italian. The ingenue was French, and the character man spoke only German. Since they couldn't understand each other, they simply waited their turn to speak. This seems to always come out all right since they make these pictures for the world market, so all the parts have to be dubbed anyway. For example, entirely in English for the English market, Spanish for the Spanish market, etc. It is very seldom in any foreign movie that the voice you hear on the sound track belongs to the actor you see on the screen.

While we were there they were doing a very sexy scene with a lot of extras. A Roman orgy! What else? As the camera panned around, a lightly clad boy extra was holding in his arms a girl wearing nothing but a veil. They'd been at it since early morning. We overhead him say to her,

"Tell me, baby, what are you doing after the orgy?"

And then as it must to all men, the time came to say "Arrivederci Roma!" We left Rome for Paris on a train. It was the same train—they just turned it around. We were told by Mary Chamberlain to watch for a Mussolini development that was being built in the thirties, abandoned because of the war and left to rot. It was not a pretty sight. All those massive modern buildings falling to dust. As we passed it we heard a child's excited voice in the next compartment . . . "Look, mommy—brand new ruins!"

CHAPTER

11 incident prone

IN THIS age of the Jet I guess Henny and I set some kind of record for continuous travel on the surface of the earth. From Rome to Paris was a repetitious rattling day-and-a-half on the train. The boat-train from Paris to Cherbourg was a hot overcrowded uncomfortable six hours. The crossing on the "Queen Mary," where we ran into a travel weary crowd and bad weather, was a very pleasant five days. But we'd had it! And the trip home on the "Twentieth Century" and the "Super Chief" was just three-and-a-half more days of iced celery, jumbo green olives, and pickled watermelon rind. So we were in constant unrelenting motion for a total of ten-and-a-half days. Ten-and-a-half days! Man, that's traveling!! Henny seemed to thrive on it. She emerged from the train looking like she'd just spent the afternoon at Elizabeth Arden's, while I staggered off bleary-eyed, rumpled, haggard and drawn, looking like the fashion editor of the *Hobo News*.

To this day I can't understand why Henny stands up

so much better than I do, since I spent the greater part of my youth on the road, and, I might add, a lot of this traveling was done in buses. This was back in the days when every two hundred miles the bus made a "comfort stop," because there was no such thing as a "comfort station" on board. Of course this is all changed nowadays. Most of your larger buses now feature indoor plumbing. I guess I have the distinction of being the first man in the history of the world ever to go to the bathroom on a bus. Let me explain!

In Hollywood everything has a premiere—meat markets, bowling alleys, pet shops, drive-in banks—you name it! These premieres usually consist of a portable bar, a battery of arc lights, some out-of-work actors, several photogenic starlets with available phone numbers and a cordon of photographers to take pictures that will never see the light of day.

Some years ago one of the bus companies inaugurated their Sceno-Cruiser Strat-O-Dome De Luxe Dread-Naught of the highways. This was the first bus ever to feature a Ladies Room and a Men's Room. So naturally, to launch this automotive and plumbing marvel, they had a traveling premiere, a junket from Los Angeles to Palm Springs, in which they included the arc lights, the "at liberty" actors, the so-called starlets, the bevy of photographers who take those pictures that never see the dark room, and out-of-work, me!

This Diesel-powered water closet took off at 9:00 in the morning. Here we were at the crack of dawn rattling down the highway with a portable bar and an accordian player. But it was 9:00 A.M. and I'm a creature of habit —so it was then that I made history! With a morning newspaper tucked underneath my arm, I made my way to the rear—the first man ever to do such a thing on board a bus!!! No . . . no, I take that back! Perhaps it had been done before on the shakedown cruise by a test pilot from Crane! Now, mind you, there I was in the powder room, happily reading my newspaper while unbeknownst to me the public relations man for the bus company who was in charge of the junket was standing up front beside the driver, facing the celebrity-studded passengers, making his inaugural spiel.

"Ladies and Gentlemen," he started, "Welcome aboard the Sceno-Cruiser! I hope you enjoy your trip, and while some of you may never travel on a bus again, still I would like to point out some of our features. First of all, there is the upper deck with its Plasti-Dome, to give you an uninterrupted view of the Burma Shave signs. And here is a really very important first—one that we're very proud of—one that really marks a milestone in highway travel— this bus is the first one, the very first one to have both a Ladies and a Gentlemen's room in the rear of the bus. This is truly a first!!!"

Now, mind you, throughout all this, I was safely ensconced in the soundproof "Gentlemen's."

"And," he continued, "this bus you are now riding in is the safest vehicle on the highway. It is equipped with the newest type of air brakes. At this moment we are cruising at 90 miles an hour. I am going to ask the driver to apply the air brakes, and believe it or not, this giant craft will come to a stop in approximately fifty feet!!! Now, before I ask the driver to apply the brakes, I must warn you . . . please brace yourselves. Each one of you, brace yourself carefully, as there will be a tremendous surge forward . . . are we ready? . . . !!"

The driver slammed on those brakes, and everything leapt forward . . . including me!! The door to the men's room flew open and I was catapulted, as I was, newspaper and all, down the whole length of the bus!!! If you think that was embarrassing, how about getting back??#@$%¢!

When we were laying over in Paris before taking the boat-train, I went shopping and bought Henny a farewell-to-Europe present. It was a beautiful thing, and she'll never get over it! So I'd better let her tell you about it.

This is Henny! By the time we finished dinner that first night on the "Queen Mary," it was almost midnight. When we got back to our quarters, lying on my bunk was a large, magnificently-wrapped box. Attached to its ribbon was an envelope which contained the following note:

> My darling,
> Thank you for the wonderful honeymoon! Remember when I disappeared during our five-day layover yesterday and refused to tell you where I was? Well, I went once again to Dior's where I had seen a lovely thing last month that reminded me of you. I should have gotten it then as they've since sold the original. But here, sweetheart, is the exact copy. It looks so like you, I couldn't get it out of my mind. Every time I looked at you in Rome, I seemed to see you in this charming negligee.
>
> Wear it for me!
Your lover

Well, of course my lover had seen me in this negligee every time he looked at me in Rome! Because I was wearing it—that's why! I was the one who bought the original. But he'll never know it from me. As a matter of fact, my sweet, darling Jimmy did the same thing to me once before—with a seven-piece solid silver tea and coffee set, no less!

It was a beautiful honeymoon—but it was nice to be going home. I felt that Jimmy was getting restless, so thank goodness we ran into some actors from back home for him to talk to. Some of the members of the "My Fair Lady" company which had just closed in Moscow were on board the "Queen Mary" with us. They were full of stories of what it was like to appear in a hit show behind the Iron Curtain.

Through Bob Coote, who played Colonel Pickering in the show, we learned something very interesting. Bob is an Englishman whose hobby is collecting broad American jokes. And here are some jokes that he told in Moscow with the aid of his interpreter:

"Did you hear about the nearsighted turtle who fell in love with an Army helmet!"

"Did you hear about the Indian who didn't know heads from tails?—He came home with some pretty funny looking scalps!!"

"Did you hear about the nearsighted whale who fell in love with a submarine and followed it clear around the world?—Every time the sub fired a torpedo, the proud whale passed out cigars!"

They even have the ability to laugh at themselves:

"Did you hear what the Russian mother said to her daughter?—Don't worry your pretty little head, my darling . . . someday, when you least expect it, along will come Mr. Left!"

The above fractured the Russians either singly or collectively—and let's face it—collectively is a very popular word in Russia. Those Russians were so grateful to Bob Coote, they told him a story . . . and here it is.

When Nikita Khrushchev visited London, the general manager of the Port of London authority was assigned to show him around. As they progressed, Mr. K. frequently stopped to question workers. Finally he came to a Dock Superintendent in charge of a crew of longshoremen unloading cargo from a ship and asked, through his interpreters:

"How many hours a day do the men work?"

"Eight," was the reply.

"*What if the ship can't be unloaded in eight hours?*" Mr. K. asked.

"*Then,*" the foreman told him, "*we ask them to work overtime. If they want to, and the union says O. K., they finish the job. If not, it has to wait until the next day.*"

"*Well,*" Mr. Khrushchev said, "*in my country we tell them to finish the job—and they do it because they know it's their duty.*"

"*Yes,*" the Dock Superintendent said, "*but you don't have a bunch of bloody Communists to deal with!*"

From the time we boarded the "Queen Mary," Jimmy was obsessed with the idea of getting up on the bridge. He's a compulsive up-fronter. He says one of the advantages of being well known is that when he gets on a plane, he sometimes is invited to sit up front with the pilot. His favorite possession in the world is a striped engineer's hat, a souvenir of a one-hundred-mile ride in the cab of my favorite train. He had sulked all the way over on the "Queen Elizabeth" because he was never invited to help the Captain steer. This time he was determined to make it.

We were having cocktails in the cabin of the Executive Officer whose friendship Jimmy had carefully cultivated. It was the last night on board—and time was running out. Nobody had asked him to help guide the liner. Finally he couldn't stand it any longer.

"I wonder if it would be possible sometime tomorrow before we land for me to pay you a visit on the bridge? You know, it's always been an ambition of mine to . . ."

The Executive Officer turned on all his Cunard charm as he interrupted him.

"We'd love to have you, old boy, but ever since the war, the line has been rather sticky about visitors up there. It's rule, you know. It's never been broken . . . except . . . there was a chap . . . what was his name?

. . . it was just a few weeks ago . . . orders from above, you know . . . now, what was his name . . . ?"

"Was it one of the Kennedy boys?" Jim asked him eagerly, "or Pandit Nehru?"

"No, no," the Executive was struggling to place it. "Oh, yes, yes, yes . . . I've got it. It was an American chap. A chemist, I believe . . . his name was . . . let's see . . . Schwab! . . . Leon Schwab! . . . that's it!! Come to think of it, he did have rather a knowledge of vessels."

"Knowledge of vessels," growled my spouse. It was plain to see that Jimmy was getting stir crazy. "The only vessels he has any knowledge of are the kind you put under a bed."

The New York skyline was even more exciting than our first glimpse of the shores of England. But later, at long last, when we got off the train at Pasadena I kind of choked up. Pasadena!—with the California sunshine! Pasadena!—with the birds coughing! Pasadena!—with the little old ladies road-racing in their Jaguars. But the most thrilling sight of all was that wonderful house of ours in Bel Air.

Is there anything more full of magic than coming home, I thought to myself? The trip was worth waiting nineteen years for—don't misunderstand me! It was perfect! It was delirious and gay and romantic . . . and all I had ever hoped for! But, oh, how good it was to be back in our own home, our own garden, our own pool, our own shining bathroom with the toilet that doesn't talk back! Just think, here I was standing in a room that didn't shake, rattle, and roll! I was home . . . and it was peaceful and beautiful. I hung my clothes on wooden hangers. I took a bath with all the hot water I could use. And I came into the bedroom . . . and there it was!!—our own great big wide wonderful king-sized bed. I could hardly wait to get into it. You know something—even the romantic French and the passionate Italians have pretty odd ideas of what a bed should be like!

That evening, after some sun and a glorious swim, we were lying in our big cool bed having delicious glasses of ice-cold Domestic champagne, when the telephone interrupted us. My husband answered . . . and under the circumstances it seemed like he talked for hours.

"Who is it?" I hissed.

"It's our agent," he said.

"Whadeesay, Whadeesay?"

"Darling," said my patient husband. "Will you please let me finish this. I wouldn't talk to him at this point . . . but it's very important. I'll tell you about it later."

Well, he did a lot of mumbling, and he finally hung up.

"O. K., Whadeesay?"

So he told me!

"Believe it or not, he was calling from Italy. While we were gone he opened an office in Rome. He says things are pretty slow here in Hollywood, but if I want to go to work right away I can do a television series in London or a picture in Paris, and he's got a great part in a movie for you in Rome. So we'd have to get back there as soon as . . ."

"What," I screamed. "Are you kidding? We're home now . . . and it's wonderful! Please tell me you're kidding!"

"All right," he laughed. "I'm kidding—I'm kidding!"

"Well, tell him, Jim . . . call him up and tell him we're staying home!"

"I don't have to," said Jimmy, pouring us each a glass of champagne. "He can't talk now anyway————" he added, giving me a little pat. "He's on a movie set in Rome but I'm going to call him back . . ."

"When?" I couldn't stand it. "When?"

"Soon, angel, soon . . . right after the orgy!"